Role conflict and the teacher

International Library of Sociology

Founded by Karl Mannheim

Editor: John Rex, University of Warwick

Arbor Scientiae
Arbor Vitae

A catalogue of the books available in the **International Library of Sociology,** and new books in preparation for the Library, will be found at the end of this volume.

Role conflict and the teacher

Gerald R. Grace

Department of Education, St Paul's College, Rugby

Routledge & Kegan Paul

London and Boston

First published 1972
by Routledge & Kegan Paul Ltd
Broadway House, 68-74 Carter Lane,
London EC4V 5EL and
9 Park Street,
Boston, Mass. 02108, U.S.A.
Printed in Great Britain by
The Lavenham Press Ltd, Lavenham, Suffolk.
© Gerald R. Grace 1972

ISBN 0 7100 7353 4

Contents

Preface

My interest in the sociology of teaching originated in studies which I undertook at the University of Exeter Institute of Education under the guidance of Dr (now Professor) Alec Ross and Mr G. W. Perry. Dr Bryan Wilson's article, 'The teacher's role: a sociological analysis',* was the specific stimulus for this research which was subsequently developed during a year as Visiting Fellow at the University of Leicester School of Education.

I am indebted to many people: to Dr Bryan Wilson for his encouragement, detailed comments on the first draft, and for permission to reproduce part of his article in the *British Journal of Sociology*, 1962; to Mr Gerald Bernbaum and the late Dr Roger Brown for valued guidance; to Professor G. H. Bantock and the Governors of St Paul's College for making possible my Visiting Fellowship. The work could not have been accomplished without the help of my colleagues, particularly George Todd and Colin Turner. My thanks are also due to the Sisters of St Paul at Leamington for providing 'sanctuary' in a noisy world. My wife has typed, talked and endured role conflict with remarkable patience and I am deeply grateful to her. Finally I am indebted to the teachers and head teachers who found time in their busy lives to assist me. I hope that this study will contribute towards a wider understanding of the complexities and conflicts of their roles.

*British Journal of Sociology, XIII (1), 1962, pp. 15-32.

Introduction

The school is a social system and in that system teachers are significant actors—yet it is remarkable what little attention is given to this fact. The sociology of teaching, with the exception of Waller's classic study, is of comparatively recent growth and has yet to emerge as a coherent and systematic field of inquiry. It can be claimed that many sociologists of education, following the earlier lead of the psychologists, have made their investigations primarily 'child-centred'. The teachers have been virtually ignored.

This book has been written as some contribution to the sociology of teaching. It has also been written from a value position which must be declared. This involves the somewhat unfashionable view that the teacher is as important as the child in the educative process and that there is as much need for systematic study of the problems and conflicts of the teacher role as of the pupil role. Waller observed that, 'most of the programs for the rehabilitation of the schools founder upon the rock of teacher resistance'.[1] The reason for this may well be that programmes of innovation which lack empirical evidence on the teacher's role, fail to chart fully the consequences of change and as a result are likely to founder. At a time of change to comprehensive school organisation, mixed ability classes and new approaches to teaching and learning, the investigation of teacher role conflicts seems a relevant activity.

This is a small scale inquiry and suffers from the limitations of such ventures. The study of one hundred and fifty secondary school teachers in a 'small town–small school' context may reveal patterns of conflict which vary considerably from those which a larger sample or a different social context might reveal. It is hoped that this investigation may stimulate further research in the field of teacher role conflict so that comparative studies are possible.

Appropriately enough the writer had to deal with his own role conflict in the process of deciding upon an orientation. Basically, this conflict arose from the realisation that whereas sociologists would legitimately expect the sociological perspective, with some concern for concepts and theoretical structure, teachers and educationalists would expect what Cicourel has called 'a common-sense definition of the world'.[2] Some attempt has been made to meet these two sets of expectations. The two opening chapters are concerned with the theoretical context of role conflict and the following seven chapters with its empirical investigation in the teaching situation. The final chapter presents a summary of conclusions and an outline of possible implications.

Considerable use has been made of material drawn from the interviews with teachers and head teachers. The inclusion of this material is seen as an essential probe into the complexities which lie behind the presentation of any statistically significant differences in patterns of conflict among various groups of teachers. As Waller remarked, 'possibly the understanding of human life will be as much advanced by the direct study of social phenomena as by the study of numerical symbols abstracted from those phenomena.'[3]

1 Approaches to the study of role conflict

Those familiar with the literature of role analysis are well acquainted with what Charters (1963) has described as 'the reigning confusion' of sociological and social psychological theory in this field. The key concepts of 'role' and 'role conflict' have been formulated in varied and sometimes contradictory ways, although important attempts have been made to produce conceptual order (see Gross *et al.* 1958; Biddle *et al.* 1966). A necessary preliminary therefore is to attempt some clarification of what can be meant by role conflict, and to outline possible reactions to it and possible consequences of unresolved role conflict.

The concept of role conflict

It is self-evident that the occupants of social and occupational roles are likely to meet with problem situations to a greater or lesser extent. These situations may arise from a variety of circumstances but the intrinsic nature of the role, the process of role performance and the context in which the role is performed will be important determinants. 'Role conflict' is the term which has been generally used by sociologists and social psychologists to denote such problem situations, although terms such as 'role strain' (Goode 1960) or 'role stress' (Westwood 1967a), which represent a particular emphasis, are also used.

Despite variations in the terms used, the central component of all of the formulations is *incompatibility*. Thus role conflict, role strain or role stress are all concerned with *problems for the individual which arise as the result of role incompatibilities.* These may take various forms—incompatibility between roles or within a specific role, incompatibility of expectations for a role or between the orientation of a role and a particular social or cultural context, incompatibility between role expectations and the personality dispositions of the individual. Incompatibilities may be seen by role occupants to be problems, or seen and felt as problems, in which case the terms 'role strain' and 'role stress' are sometimes used to denote degrees of personal concern. As Kahn *et al.* (1964) point out, it is possible to examine role conflict 'as a fact in the environment of the person and as a fact in his internal, psychological life'.[1]

Strategies and categories

Role conflict studies adopt various approaches to the examination of role incompatibilities. Some are concerned with conflict which is seen to exist in a situation by an outside observer. This is sometimes referred to as objective role conflict. Thus Seeman's (1953) analysis of the school superintendent's role focuses on 'situations in which the observer notes what appear to be conflicting sets of expectations'.[2]

Theoretical analysis of role conflict has been much influenced by the application of Talcott Parsons's (1951) 'pattern variables' to various role situations. Role occupants are seen to be faced with potential conflict arising out of value choices which they have to make. Important among these are the extent to which they become emotionally involved in role relationships (affectivity *v.* affectivity neutrality); the extent to which they put their own interests before those of the group or organisation (self-orientation *v.* collectivity orientation) and the extent to which they employ universal standards in specific local situations (universalism *v.* particularism). Wilson's (1962) important and influential analysis of teacher role conflicts centres around the 'pattern variable' dilemmas.

Empirical studies are of two main categories. *Perceptual studies* attempt to measure the role occupant's perception of conflicting expectations or orientations. It is clear that while a social situation may be one which to the observer is charged with conflict, the role occupants may or may not perceive this. Studies in this category characteristically ask the occupants of roles to rate the expectations which they perceive as being held for their role by 'significant others'. Role conflict is said to exist when there are important differences among the ratings given for various expectations. In a recent study, Musgrove (1967) asked groups of teachers to rank four main aspects of the teacher's role (discipline, teaching, personality and organisation) as they ideally valued them and as they thought the head of the school, their colleagues, parents and pupils respectively valued them. By comparing the extent of agreement or disagreement among the ranks, a measure of role conflict was obtained. Perceptual studies have been strongly criticised for presenting an over-simplified and mis-leading concept of role conflict, by those who believe that the simple perception of divergent expectations cannot be said to constitute conflict.[3]

The work of Getzels and Guba (1954) has been important for stressing the need to go beyond simple perception of incompatibil-ities to consider the extent to which such situations actually trouble role occupants. *Perceptual–experiential studies* attempt to measure degrees of affective concern over incompatibilities and to relate these to certain characteristics of the role occupant, including personality variables. Gross *et al.* (1958), for instance, have investigated the extent to which school superintendents were concerned about incompatibilities in their role and Kahn *et al.* (1964) have developed similar inquiries in an industrial setting.

A major distinction in role conflict studies has been made between *inter-role conflicts* and *intra-role conflicts*. The former, according to Sarbin (1954), 'occur when a person occupies two or more positions simultaneously and when the role expectations of one are incompatible with the role expectations of the other.'[4] A classic example is the conflict which can arise for the professional man between meeting fully the expectations for his professional role and meeting fully the expectations for other social roles such as those of husband and father. Studies have been made of the inter-role conflict of such vulnerable positions as the military chaplain (Burchard 1954) and the teacher in America (Getzels and Guba 1955). The recent emphasis of research has, however,

3

tended to shift from inter-role to intra-role conflict, i.e. to an interest in conflict arising (from a number of sources) within a specific role.

In the investigation of role conflict, sociologists have concentrated their attention on determinants of conflict arising from the *context* in which a role is performed, while psychologists have concentrated upon the characteristics of the *person* occupying the role. The sociological perspective emphasises the cultural and societal setting of a role, the inter-relationships between a role and various organisational settings and the articulation of a role in a network of other roles. Psychologists, on the other hand, emphasise the expectations and perceptions of the individual performing the role, and emphasise also the importance of personality characteristics as factors in role conflict. There is, as a consequence, a good deal of overlap among the various formulations of role conflict. They represent not so much analytically distinct categories but rather problem situations viewed from different perspectives and with different emphases.

Role–culture conflict

Conflict from this viewpoint is seen in terms of basic dis-harmony between the essential commitments of particular roles and the culture or ethos in which they are performed. It is claimed (Reisman *et al.* 1950, Floud 1962, Wilson 1962) that roles having a moral and ethical orientation and which are concerned with the transmission of values, are exposed to considerable conflict in the cultures of advanced industrial societies. This conflict arises because of the breakdown of value consensus, because of changed attitudes to authority and because of the growth of hedonistic and other-directed philosophies of life. Certain roles are seen to be in a 'confrontation position' with the developing tendencies of the culture and the teacher's role is characteristically regarded as one of these.

Role–organisation conflict

A good deal of attention has focused on the characteristics of organisations as determinants of role conflict (see Katz and Kahn

1966). The number of variables in this area is considerable. Leadership styles, goal setting and goal attainment, work climate, allocation of resources, communication patterns, specialisation and co-ordination, organisational commitment and professional orientation, characteristics of the clientele and relationships with the external environment have to be considered in relation to the role conflicts of individuals within organisations. In particular, attention has focused on the conflicts of professional workers in bureaucratic organisations, where the professional orientation stressing autonomy, quality of service and the application of universalistic criteria may clash with bureaucratic requirements stressing supervision and uniformity, routine and particularistic criteria.[5] Role-organisation conflict is seen to be a major category for teachers in America (Corwin 1965) and it has been suggested that the growing size and bureaucratisation of schools in this country may soon create similar problems for British teachers (Hoyle 1965; Westwood 1967b).

Role–community conflict

The community context of a role is always an important dimension to be considered in conflict analysis. Conflict for the occupants of certain roles can arise when community expectations for the role are powerful and prescriptive and run counter to those of the role occupant. This is another area of conflict which has been regarded as a major category for teachers in America, where such influences on both the teacher's private life in the community and his professional life in the school have been strong. Such problem situations have been analysed by a long line of American studies, starting with Waller's influential work in 1932.[6] A further potential area of role-community conflict relates to the social class variable. If social class groups are viewed as representing broadly different sub-cultures, with different life styles, sets of assumptions and patterns of values and aspirations, then the potential conflict of a 'middle-class' role in a working-class community becomes apparent. This is especially so if the 'middle-class' role is attempting to change life styles, assumptions, values and aspirations embedded in the community. Incompatibilities arise for the role occupant because of divergent cultural and value orientations of the role and of the immediate community setting. Recent work in this country (Musgrove and Taylor 1969) has underlined the importance of the immediate social context as a factor in role conflict analysis.

Role–role set conflict

An individual usually has a reasonably clear idea of how his role should be performed but it is apparent that no role exists in a social vacuum. Each role is articulated in a network of other roles representing positions with which the individual interacts. This network of roles is referred to as the 'role set' and is defined by Merton (1957) as, 'that complement of role relationships which persons have by virtue of occupying a particular social status'.[7] Thus the role of the teacher may be seen as part of a network in which the roles of pupil, headteacher, head of department, colleague, parent and HMI are important positions in the role set.

Each position in the role set may be regarded as having expectations* for the role and these expectations may not agree, with the result that a potential role conflict situation is created for the 'focal person'. Conflict may arise because the individual 'perceives that others hold different expectations for him as the incumbent of a single position'[8] or because the expectations of one or more members of the role set conflict with the individual's own role conception. A teacher, for instance, may find himself at the focal point of expectations from parents that he should concentrate on basic subjects and examination successes. These expectations may conflict with those from a 'progressive' head teacher or HMI that he should concentrate on personality development and wider cultural horizons. Both of these sets of expectations may conflict with his own 'middle of the road' role concept. Gross et al. (1958) have suggested that in advanced societies roles cannot be regarded in a consensus framework but must be seen rather as 'sets of expectations' for various social positions. The concept of a role as a set of expectations can clearly result in many formulations of role conflict depending upon the position studied, the population involved and the range of expectations examined.[9]

---

*Expectations are standards of evaluation concerned with how a role should be performed and what should be the attributes of role occupants (see Gross et al. 1958).

Self-role or person-role conflict

The emphasis in the definition of self-role or person-role conflict is upon the individual performing the role rather than upon the context in which it is performed. Two major categories of self-role conflict may be distinguished; the first concerns incompatibilities between the expectations which an occupant may have for a role and the actual perceptions* which he has of the role. It is essentially conflict between the ideal and the actual. An individual may feel that a role, because of its complexity and the significance of its activity for the social system, should be highly regarded (characteristically—should be accorded professional status). His perception may be, that this is far from being the case and that the role is regarded as unimportant and commonplace. In this way, a potential role conflict situation[10] is created for the individual, which may in this case show itself in what has been described as 'status anxiety' or 'status insecurity'. It is clear that ideal-actual conflict is likely to be present in many roles, particularly where evaluation and reward of the role are being considered or when ideal and actual role performance are examined (Burnham 1964).

A second category of conflict, where the emphasis is upon the individual, concerns incompatibilities which may arise between the expectations held for a role by the individual or others and the personality dispositions of the role occupants. Getzels and Guba (1957) have pointed out, that role expectations and personality needs both have a quality of demand upon the person and these demands may be incompatible. In this case, 'if the institutional demands (or it could be added—"role demands") are contradictory to, or irrelevant to, the demands of personality, then the individual is presented with a conflict'.[11] So, for instance, a teacher with personality dispositions towards assertion and exhibition may face a conflict in a situation organised for 'learning experiences' where the emphasis is upon democratic group procedures and the self-effacement of the teacher. Similarly, roles which are essentially diffuse in obligation and intangible in results may precipitate problems for certain personality types.

*It is important to note that these perceptions may not be accurate.

Resolution of role conflict

Role occupants who are faced with role conflict situations which trouble them can naturally be expected to attempt some resolution of the conflict. The approach which an individual may adopt will depend upon the nature and intensity of the conflict, the situational setting and certain characteristics of the person.

Redefinition of the situation

In this case, conflict acts as stimulus to the role occupant to attempt to change the situation in which he finds troubling incompatibilities. For instance, a teacher in conflict with the bureaucratic requirements of a school may seek formally to reduce the number of regulations or the amount of paper work. He may, in addition, stress the importance of professional autonomy and of individual discretionary powers and work to have these concepts 'written in' to the school's procedure (he may of course informally ignore as many bureaucratic requirements as possible!). Similarly, teachers troubled by perceived lack of status for their profession or for their particular expertise (e.g. teacher of infants) may as a consequence engage in types of action designed to change this situation. Getzels (1963) has stressed that 'certain types of conflict, like certain types of necessity, give rise to productive transformations',[12] and it is clear that what may be described as positive reaction to conflict situations, provides the dynamic for much organisational and social change.

Adaptation to incompatible expectations

When a role occupant is faced with incompatible expectations and assuming that he does not reject all expectations other than his own, then some strategy of adaptation is required. He may adopt an 'expedient orientation' (Gross *et al.* 1958) and resolve the conflict by conforming to the expectations of those whom he perceives as significant, whom he wishes to impress or whose sanctions he fears (this might be termed the Uriah Heep response).

In contrast to this, a role occupant may ignore the significance-power dimension and take a 'moral orientation' to the situation, concentrating upon the question of the legitimacy of expectations for the role and rejecting those which appear illegitimate, regardless of the source (the Sir Thomas More response). A third possibility would involve the adoption of a 'moral-expedient' orientation where the role occupant attempts to balance legitimate expectations with considerations of his own self-interest (the 'average man' response). It is also possible, as Merton (1957) has pointed out, for a role occupant to make the members of his role set aware of the incompatible expectations which they have for the role and in this way to encourage them to resolve the situation themselves.

The perceived legitimacy of expectations held for a role is a crucial factor in the formation of an individual's role concept and in the resolution of role conflict situations. The more expectations which are accepted by a role occupant as legitimate, the greater the role 'load' and the greater the potentiality for conflict.[13] A teacher who accepts expectations that he should act as socialiser, counsellor and liaison between home and school as well as director of learning, as being legitimate, clearly has more sources for strain in the role than a teacher who accepts as legitimate only the expectation that he should be a director of learning. There is some evidence that secondary modern school teachers accept the legitimacy of a wider range of expectations than grammar school teachers (Musgrove and Taylor 1969) and this has implications for their vulnerability to role conflict.

If none of these techniques is appropriate, then the role occupant can be expected to attempt to compromise, but this may be highly demanding of energy and lead to feelings of dissatisfaction. For instance, a teacher attempting to keep up with new developments in his subject and at the same time attempting to play a full part in extra-curricular activities, may be in this situation. Getzels and Guba (1954) have suggested that in such a situation a role occupant will tend to commit himself to a major role 'in order to determine his action at choice points'.[14] The teacher may thus resolve the problem by committing himself to a major academic role and a minor extra-curricular role (or vice versa). The choice of major role, according to Getzels and Guba, will be influenced by the personality needs of the individual as well as by the legitimacy of expectations.

Role retreatism

It is possible to resolve role conflict situations by actions which essentially involve a retreat from the role. Intensity of role conflict experience is known to be related to the degree to which an individual commits himself to a role (Katz and Kahn 1966). By reducing commitment to the role, creating a psychological distance or finding alternative reference groups, a role occupant can thereby reduce the intensity of experienced role conflict. In everyday terms, the individual is observed to lose interest in the activities of the role.

A similar, though less global, process occurs when a role occupant abandons a particular set of expectations or a particular orientation for a role as a result of certain experiences. For instance, the teacher may feel that he should widen the cultural horizons of his pupils or change their values in certain ways. His perception may be that his attempts to do so over the years are apparently fruitless. In this situation he may retreat from his original role concept, resolving the conflict by claiming that certain activities are impossible with a particular group of pupils. Role retreatism does not necessarily always imply defeat. It may involve a strategic withdrawal from untenable positions which not only resolves conflict but improves the effectiveness of the role occupant. Floud (1962) has suggested that teachers must retreat from a missionary orientation in their role to a social worker orientation if they are to be effective in modern society. From this point of view, role retreatism involves functional adaptation to changed circumstances. On the other hand, certain types of role retreatism occurring over time may be associated with pessimism, lack of idealism and flexibility in role occupants. An extreme case of role retreatism, as a result of conflict situations, involves an occupant in what Toby (1952) has called 'escape from the field'.[15] In an attempt to escape from role conflict pressures, an individual may move to another organisation or may abandon the role altogether.

Broadly speaking, therefore, attempts to resolve role conflict may take the form of positive, adaptive or retreatist reactions. Exposed to role conflict in the teaching situation, one teacher can become a militant reformer, determined to change certain circumstances in the situation, another can resolve the incompatibilities by a system of priorities or compromises, while a third can become disengaged and pessimistic about the whole business. Some writers suggest[16] that teachers in the past have been too willing to make adaptive or retreatist reactions to conflict situations. If this has been true, current signs of militancy among teachers both in Britain and America would suggest that this pattern is changing.

Consequences of role conflict

Although various resolution techniques exist for individuals in role conflict situations, it cannot be assumed that these are always operative or always effective and therefore certain role occupants will continue to be exposed to on-going conflict. The consequences of unresolved role conflict will vary with the type and intensity of conflict, the context in which it is found, and the characteristics of the individual exposed to it. In some cases, as already suggested, conflict can be functional to the individual, the organisation or the society, acting as a stimulus to the analysis of problems and a motive force behind programmes of change and reform. Coser (1956) in *The Functions of Social Conflict* has argued that 'a flexible society benefits from conflict because such behaviour, by helping to create and modify norms, assures its continuance under changed conditions'.[17] Similar arguments can be advanced in considering the functions of certain types of conflict for roles and organisations. It could be argued, for instance, that certain role conflicts created for teachers by the diffuse objectives of post-war secondary modern schools (Taylor 1963) were responsible, with other forces, for the dynamic towards external examinations and visible results. This development in turn helped to assure the continuance of the secondary modern school as an organisation against the arguments of comprehensive school supporters concerning lack of opportunity in such schools.

More attention has been given to the dysfunctional consequences of role conflict. This appears to be due to the preoccupation of many sociologists with equilibrium and adjustment in social systems (Coser 1956; Buckley 1967). The influence of the sociological theories of Talcott Parsons has been important in this respect. From this viewpoint role conflict is seen as disruptive and tension inducing, with adverse effects both for the role occupants and the organisation of which he is a member. Clearly, certain types of conflict at certain intensities 'will exact a price, both in terms of individual well-being and organisational effectiveness'.[18] The 'price' may be reduction of commitment or abandonment of certain objectives by the individual (role retreatism), reduced satisfaction with a role in a particular situation (job dissatisfaction) or in any situation (career dissatisfaction), or increased personal strain and anxiety. It is also argued that high levels of unresolved role conflict can affect the actual role performance of an individual, leading to lower levels of competence and effectiveness. Empirical evidence exists to support some of these assertions. Gross *et al.* (1958), in studying the conflicts of school superintendents, found that perceived role conflict was associated with lower job satisfaction. Kahn *et al.* (1964) found that intensity of experienced role conflict was associated with job-related tensions, lower job satisfaction and reduced confidence in superiors and the organisation as a whole. It must be said, however, that relatively little empirical investigation has been made of the possibly functional effects of certain types of role conflict.

In the teaching situation, unresolved role conflict can have a number of effects. It may activate some teachers to press for change in the curriculum, the organisation of schools or the structure of the profession. It may, on the other hand, be responsible for a situation where 'the teacher is likely to belittle the accomplishments of education and to take a cynical attitude towards his work, the school system and educational ideas and ideals'.[19]

2 The teacher and role conflict

The teacher's role is widely regarded as a classic conflict situation. Potentiality for conflict has been suggested from a variety of sources—the diffuse nature of the role (Wilson 1962), teachers' concern with status (Tropp 1957), their exposure to conflicting expectations (Merton 1957), the affectivity and moral orientation of the role (Floud 1962; Wilson 1962) and characteristics of the organisational setting (Corwin 1965; Hoyle 1965). Westwood (1967 b, p. 24), in applying 'pattern variable' analysis to the teacher's role, has suggested that, 'in the teacher's role, the dilemmas stemming from the pattern variables are found in an acuter form than in most other occupational roles'. If role conflict means 'problems for the individual', then at first sight teachers would appear to have more than their fair share of problems!

Such a general conclusion, however, can be misleading, since it fails to take into account a number of important qualifications which have to be made. The first is that while *potentiality* for conflict has been outlined for the teacher's role in various theoretical analyses, empirical evidence is not always available to confirm or deny actual conflict. While some important American work does exist, Musgrove and Taylor (1969, p. 8), summing up the situation in this country, have claimed that 'the role of the teacher in modern society has proved an inexhaustible subject for arm-chair theorizing and inaugural lectures. There are virtually no empirical studies of the contemporary role of teachers.'

A further important qualification involves the distinction of cultural settings in teacher role studies. While there are certain continuities in the position of the teacher in Britain and America, there are also significant differences (Baron and Tropp 1961). Major categories of role conflict for teachers in America may have very little relevance to teachers in Britain. It is also apparent that the use of the term 'teacher' begs many questions. The occupational category of teacher, which can extend from the infant school to the university, probably encompasses a wider range of role settings, role conceptions and role activities than many other occupational groups. To talk of role conflict in the teaching situation is consequently a hazardous undertaking unless related to specific teacher roles.[1] This chapter will examine categories of objective role conflict for teachers which have been suggested in theoretical analysis and it will examine also British and American evidence relating to these categories. Presentation will centre upon the work of Wilson (1962), whose analysis of teacher role conflicts has exercised a considerable influence upon all subsequent work in this area.

Wilson has suggested (1962, p. 27) that 'all roles in which there is a high commitment to other people are subject to considerable internal conflicts and insecurities' and his specific focus is upon those conflicts which are 'intrinsic to the teacher's role and the circumstances in which it is performed'. He identifies six possible categories of role conflict for teachers.

Conflict arising from the diffuse nature of the teacher's role

In Wilson's view (1962, p. 22), the teacher's role necessarily has a diffuse rather than a specific commitment—'the business of socializing children, of motivating, inspiring and encouraging them, of transmitting values to them, awakening in them a respect for facts and a sense of critical appreciation—all of this is unspecific. It implies "what a man is" as much as "what a man does".' The problem which arises for the teacher from this viewpoint relates to the question of knowledge of results. While the academic sector of the teacher's work provides some tangible evidence of achievement (or lack of it), the wider areas of role commitment which have to do with changes in pupils' interests, behaviours, attitudes and values, may give little or no indication of what has been achieved. Thus a role which demands considerable investment of self by its practitioners may provide only a limited sense of achievement. The question 'What has been accomplished?' can be a crucial one for the teacher, the social worker or the priest, and it may be an important source of conflict. As Wilson puts it (1962, p. 27), 'diffuse roles are likely to embody internal role conflicts because of the absence of clear lines of demarcation whereby the role player knows when he has "done his job".' Making the assumption that individuals need to know how successful they are in a particular role and what they are achieving in role performance, conflict for teachers in this area might be more closely defined as, incompatibility between the individual's need to see the results of role performance and the 'invisibility' of many of the results of teacher role performance.

That role diffuseness or role ambiguity[2] is productive of conflict and strain for some role occupants has been shown by Wardwell (1955) and Kahn *et al.* (1964), but there is little evidence that teachers see or feel a problem in this area. It may be that they resolve any possible conflict by accepting as inevitable, intangibility of achievement in certain areas of their work or they may avoid the conflict by defining their role narrowly in terms which are largely measurable.

While no empirical work in this country has investigated teacher role diffuseness, two very articulate but atypical teachers have asserted emphatically that there is a problem. D. H. Lawrence, reflecting on his brief teaching experience, felt that 'you never know what you have done or if you have really done anything. Manual work is much more satisfying. You can see something for all your pains. You know whether you have done a job well or not, but with teaching you never know.'[3] A. S. Neill has written: 'most teachers have a more or less vague feeling that their work is pouring water down a drain. His work is psychically much more exhausting than that of a lawyer or a doctor...because he has a job that never finishes, a job in which he can never see the end.'[4]

On the other hand, Gerstl (1967) has argued that 'the ambiguity or possible role conflict stemming from the diffuse nature of the socializing function (of teachers) is unlikely to be a major source of strain in itself',[5] and Miles (1969) found that even the suggestion that 'it is difficult to know when you are doing a good job' was rejected almost unanimously by the teachers and principals whom he interviewed.[6] Peterson (1964), however, as a result of his interviews with women high-school teachers in America, came to the conclusion that role diffuseness was an important problem for teachers.

It is apparent then that no clear picture exists at present of the degree to which teachers see a problem of intangibility or diffuseness in their role, or the degree to which they are troubled by possible role ambiguity and more research in this area is required.

Conflicts of the teacher role set

Wilson believes that 'the role-set of the teacher is especially formidable because the role is diffuse and because everyone in contemporary society has ready opinions about what the teacher does and should do'.[7] The teacher is thus seen to be at the focus of conflicting expectations concerning how his role should be performed, and the role is seen to be vulnerable to outside influences because teachers 'cannot protect their role by jargon or by the use of dead language as doctors or lawyers do'.[8]

The teacher, vulnerable to conflicting expectations, is a familiar theme in role analysis, especially in American studies. Merton (1957), in developing the theory of conflict in the role set, took the position of the teacher in America as a model:[9]

the teacher may thus become subject to conflicting role expectations among such members of his role set as professional colleagues, influential members of the school board and, say, the Americanism Committee of the American Legion. What is an educational essential for the one, may be judged an education frill, or as downright subversion by the other. These disparate and contradictory evaluations by members of the role-set greatly complicate the task of coping with them all. The familiar case of the teacher may be taken as paradigmatic. What holds conspicuously for this one status, holds in varying degrees for the occupants of all other statuses.

This situation clearly reflects the closer community involvement in school affairs which is traditional in America and it reflects also the potential pressures that can come to bear upon the teacher from various sources.

A good deal of empirical work has consequently examined this type of role conflict for the American teacher (Charters 1963). This work has shown that teachers perceive exposure to conflicting expectations (Manwiller 1958) and are troubled by them (Getzels and Guba 1955) but there is evidence also which suggests that much of this conflict is 'in the eye of the beholder' rather than in actuality. The work of Biddle and others (1964) has drawn attention to the possibility of misperception of expectations, i.e. that teachers see more conflict in expectations for their role than actually exists among members of their role set or between the role set and their own role conception.

Investigation of conflicts of the role set for teachers in Britain is of comparatively recent date. Burnham (1964), as part of a wider examination of the position of the deputy head in secondary schools, investigated expectations for the role as perceived by the occupants. He found that deputy heads in secondary modern schools, particularly small schools, saw themselves exposed to significantly more conflict stemming from divergent expectations of the head and the teachers, than did grammar-school deputy heads. The position of the deputy head has been regarded as particularly vulnerable to role conflict by virtue of his 'man in the middle' position. Burnham's findings indicated that type of school and size of school were important variables affecting actual exposure to role conflict although reasons for the greater vulnerability of the role in the secondary modern school remain speculative.

A series of studies by Musgrove and Taylor provide the main source of evidence relating to teacher role conflict in this country. This work reveals the way in which a teacher's concept of his role (and hence his potential exposure to role conflict) varies with type of school (infant, junior, modern, grammar) and with the social context of the school defined in terms of social class. It also indicates that teachers see more conflict between their role priorities and those which they attribute to parents, than is the case empirically. The suggestion is made that, 'on the whole, teachers take an unflattering view of parents...in fact parents were substantially in agreement with teachers. The area of (unnecessary) tension might be considerably reduced if parents and teachers established more effective means of communication.'[10]

Subsequent work (Musgrove 1967) investigated the perceived role conflict of secondary-school teachers arising from different evaluations of four areas of the teacher's role (discipline, teaching, personality, organisation) by various members of the role set. It was found that there was a greater proportion of teachers in high conflict in secondary modern schools than in grammar schools and this was attributed to the less established position of the secondary modern school as an institution and to its still uncertain objectives. The major source of conflict for nearly all the teachers in the inquiry was the perceived expectations of the head teachers. The head was seen as placing great emphasis on discipline when assistants would place it elsewhere.

Conflicts of infant and junior school teachers have been examined along similar lines, but special attention has been paid to the social class composition of the school's catchment area (Taylor 1968). The social context of the school defined in these terms has been found to be a major variable in determining exposure to role conflict—'Teachers, whether men or women, no matter what their age or length of teaching experience, if they were teaching in junior schools serving a predominantly working class catchment area, were in higher conflict about their role as teachers than their colleagues in schools serving a mixed or mainly middle class area.'[11] In their most recent study (essentially a presentation of earlier work), Musgrove and Taylor (1969) have called for more research into the consequences for teacher role conflict of such changes as comprehensive school reorganisation, predicting that grammar-school teachers are likely to develop sharper role conflicts as a result of changed expectations and role settings.

Conflict arising from the characteristics of schools as institutions

The vulnerability of the teacher's role to external pressures is, in Wilson's view, emphasised by the vulnerability of the institutions in which the role is performed. Schools and their personnel are seen to be much more exposed to public pressure than are hospitals, courts or universities and their personnel, and the influence of laymen upon decision-making in education is regarded as an important limitation upon the professionalism of teachers. Wilson asserts that, 'of all professions, teachers have least control of the institution in which their role is performed.'[12] Conflict for teachers in this situation can arise because they perceive that institutional arrangements, and the general way in which they are treated in the society, do not accord with their desired professional status and self-image. The concern of teachers about their professional status has been widely commented upon in both Britain and America (Charters 1963; Westwood 1967a) and research has shown that certain categories of teacher in both countries are subject to status-anxiety (Lieberman 1956; Tropp 1957). Much of the research, however, is general in conception and few studies are specifically concerned with relating the variables of professional status and institutional vulnerability.

The importance of considering teacher role conflicts in relation to certain organisational characteristics of schools has been emphasised by Hoyle (1965) but empirical work in Britain is still sparse.[13] The existence of considerably more American work (Corwin 1965; Carver and Sergiovanni 1969) can be attributed partly to the fact that the vulnerability of the teacher's role and of the school as an institution is clearly more of a problem than in Britain. Corwin argues that 'the position of educators in the American schools is one that is especially vulnerable to role conflicts' and that this is particularly so in relation to 'the efforts of teachers to carve out a professional status amidst the growing inroads of complex bureaucracies.'[14] A major area of role conflict for the teacher in America arises out of the clash between the long-standing tradition of the teacher as a salaried employee of the community and local public servant and the aspiration of many teachers[15] for professional status involving greater auton-omy and cosmopolitan rather than local standards and values. The struggle of American teachers to assert professional in-dependence and autonomy from the community is complicated by the increasingly bureaucratic nature of American schools. Bureaucratisation is seen as reinforcing the employee status of teachers by emphasising standardisation of procedures and restricting the area of professional autonomy.[16] The drive towards professionalism by teachers and the development of increased bureaucratisation in schools (often, but not always, related to greater size) represent powerful forces containing considerable potential for conflict. In Corwin's view, this problem is central to the American educational scene.

It seems unlikely that this type of role conflict exists in Britain to anything like the extent claimed for American teachers. The greater isolation of the teacher and the school from community pressures, the professional prestige of academic specialisms, the generally smaller size of schools and the acceptance of considerable autonomy for teachers within the schools, create radically different conditions. The teacher in Britain, it has been suggested, has more of the 'despot' tradition than of the public servant tradition, and is seen as enjoying extensive freedom from bureaucratic restraints—

> he is free to respond or not to respond as he thinks fit. He is particularly jealous of his freedom from both ministerial and parental 'interference' with regard to the curriculum; his resistance to 'dinner duty' symbolizes his determination to exclude the tasks of social welfare from his role. In fact the teacher in the maintained schools insists on a special, even a privileged position, among professional workers in contemporary Britain.[17]

To what extent this situation will change as the result of the increasing size of schools, changing patterns of internal organisation, new approaches to teaching and the growing emphasis on closer home-school relationships, is difficult to predict. The larger size of educational units may precipitate certain conflicts for teachers arising out of bureaucratic requirements or out of a more impersonal atmosphere. Parental 'power' may for the first time begin to make an impact on the schools as greater numbers of well-educated parents with higher expectations and increased confidence are encouraged to participate more closely in educational affairs. Open plan classrooms, team teaching and similar developments which affect an increasing number of teachers may provoke strains arising from altered role settings. In short, the changing characteristics of schools both internally and in their external relationships may expose teachers in Britain to role conflicts from which previously they have been shielded.

Conflict of role commitment and career orientation in teaching

The clarification of this suggested role conflict for teachers is skilfully developed in Wilson's analysis[18] and is substantially reproduced here:

> Because of the diffuse, affective character of the teaching role there is in contemporary society a most significant role conflict arising from the divergence of role commitment and career orientation. The teacher is—like everyone in contemporary society—exposed to the pressure to 'get on'. Achievement and social mobility are the accepted cultural goals of our society and there are well-structured systems of inducement to motivate men to these ends. Yet the teaching role demands the cultivation of sustained relationships with particular children, and this necessarily means a continued commitment to a particular situation. But the teacher, and particularly the young teacher, ought to want to 'move on to a better job', according to our widely accepted social values. If this is not a possibility, he should want to improve himself in other ways—to move to more congenial schools. There is a considerable horizontal mobility as well as vertical mobility in the teaching profession. Teachers prefer better surroundings, more teachable and brighter children, fewer problems of discipline and yet the need for committed people as teachers and as models is evident. If teachers are 'on the move' the affective aspects of their role are less well performed, they become impersonal transmitters of skills who do not know their children and whose children do not know them—sometimes not even by name. The damage done by high teacher turnover has not been assessed and yet a frequent excuse by children and head teachers for poor performance is the fact that there has been a change of teachers. Often the least attractive schools with the need for the highest commitment

suffer most. Thus it is that the career line which the young teacher is expected to desire is in fact a career line which cuts across the commitment to his role. It means reduced loyalty to the institution of which he is a part, to the clientele whom he serves—especially so since his service is of its very nature particularistic. But it is evident that colleagues and the world at large judge the individual in terms of his career line rather than in terms of the care, concern and commitment which are involved in role performance. These are largely unseen and in a highly mobile society are likely to be seen less and less. There is an inducement in this situation to make right impressions on the significant people rather than significant impressions on the right people—the children. Financial security, social prestige, one's own self-esteem, once these values have been completely internalized they are reflected more and more in the capacity to 'get on' rather than to do the job well. Indeed, inability to do well in the role may itself be an inducement to further mobility: the less role committed can become the more career oriented and the less adequate teachers can accept the incentive to get ahead more easily than the intensely role committed. In an inner-directed society the satisfactions of good performance of the role would be sufficient; once men are 'other-directed' they become more concerned with success as acknowledged by others rather than with their own knowledge of their good performance.

The power of this argument stems from the fact that it deals with one of the most fundamental role conflict situations which men encounter—that between self-interest and the interests of others. It is suggested that this conflict, always present in society, has become intensified in modern industrial societies where visible success and public recognition have heightened significance, where greater opportunities exist for job mobility and social mobility and where growing secularisation weakens the belief that God, even if no one else, sees the dedication of individuals. This latter argument, is used by Sir Thomas More (in Robert Bolt's play, *A Man for All Seasons*) to persuade Richard Rich to become a teacher:

More Why not be a teacher? You'd be a fine teacher. Perhaps a great one.
Rich And if I was, who would know it?
More You, your pupils, your friends, God—not a bad audience that.

It is significant that this argument failed to convince Richard Rich.

Conflict between role commitment and career orientation is clearly not confined to the teaching situation. Ben-David (1958) has analysed the conflicts of doctors arising from their commitment to their patients, in the form of quality of service given, and their realisation that advancement in their profession is related to research activity and publication. What is argued by Wilson is that this type of conflict is particularly severe for teachers because of the importance of affective commitment in the role—'the strictly professional attitude—to remember that one's clients are just cases—so much stressed in medicine, law and social work, is simply not possible in teaching.'[19]

There can be no doubt that the importance of relationships, of rapport and of 'real liking for children' are central to the culture of teacher education in Britain as represented by the colleges of education and central to the socialisation of non-graduate students for the teacher's role. Insofar as the colleges of education have a professional concept of the teacher's role, it is one which, unlike many professional concepts, stresses the necessity of sustained and warm relationships with the client. The socialisation of graduate students within university departments of education follows on the other hand the more traditional professional pattern of affective neutrality (Taylor 1969a). It seems likely therefore that these two contrasting patterns of socialisation will affect the vulnerability of different categories of teacher to conflicts of role commitment and career orientation. It can be expected that certificated teachers from colleges of education will both perceive and experience higher role conflict in this area than graduate teachers from university departments of education, since the importance of relationships and commitment will be more central to the role concepts of the former. While a good deal of informal comment upon this type of role conflict exists in many school staffrooms, and while it probably provides much of the dynamic behind teacher dissatisfaction with the promotion structure in teaching, no systematic research has been undertaken.

Few American studies appear to bear directly upon this type of role conflict. Career mobility and career aspiration of teachers have been examined (Becker 1952b; Herriott *et al.* 1966) but without reference to role conflict. Considerable interest has however been shown in conflict where the emphasis is upon the clash between organisational, rather than client, commitment and the professional orientation of various role occupants (Blau and Scott 1963). The findings of these studies indicate the complexity of factors involved in conflict between commitment (organisational or client) and the professional or career orientations of individuals, involving as they do an examination of concepts of professionalism, the structure of organisations and analysis of human motivation.

Value conflicts

In both Britain and America, teachers have in the past been expected to exhibit religious and moral virtues in their own person (the teacher as value model) and expected to transmit these virtues to their pupils (the teacher as value bearer). These values have essentially involved a moral–religious component emphasising consideration for others, honesty and truthfulness and the importance of 'spiritual' as opposed to 'material' impulses—and a social-cultural component emphasising good manners, respect for persons and property, thrift, independence and initiative with responsibility, constructive use of leisure, ambition and the work-success ethic. As the history of the profession shows, a teacher's moral and spiritual standing and his value commitments were for long regarded as of more consequence than his intellectual or academic ability—indeed if the latter was of high quality it might be regarded with suspicion, as likely to be detrimental to 'goodness' (Tropp 1957). The function of teachers in both countries was partly that of 'missionary' in so far as they took a gospel of religious and social values from the enlightened section of society to the unenlightened (Floud 1962)—and partly that of 'agent of social cohesion' in so far as they sought to maintain or promote consensus on value questions (Taylor 1969a). Far-reaching changes in modern industrial societies have, according to a number of observers, caused severe problems in this area of the teacher's role. In Wilson's view, the growth of pluralism in values has created a conflict situation for the teacher, especially so since the alternative or 'new' values are 'frequently presented in terms of the values of youth against those of age—and the teacher is clearly represented as the voice of the past.'[20] Floud (1962) has argued that the affluent society 'precipitates a crisis in the teacher's role which is a familiar feature of the American scene and in this country is incipient and potentially severest in the secondary school'.[21] This crisis is seen to arise as the result of declining respect for institutional authority and a widening social and spiritual gulf between generations which together undermine the moral authority of the teacher. From this viewpoint the mass media and the peer group are seen as powerful sources of alternative values to those of the teacher.

A similar theme can be traced in Reisman *et al.* (1950) and in Spindler (1963). Spindler has claimed that a major shift in American values is taking place, represented by a move from 'traditional' to 'emergent' values. Traditional values are conceived of as puritan morality: respectability, thrift, self-denial, sexual constraint, work-success ethic, individualism, achievement orientation and future-time orientation (present needs must be denied for satisfactions to be gained in the future). Emergent values are conceived of as sociability, relativistic moral attitudes, consideration for others, hedonistic present time orientation (no one can tell what the future will hold, therefore one should enjoy the present) and conformity to the group. In Spindler's view, it is the older teacher who, being more likely to have internalised traditional values than the younger teacher, will be exposed to potentially severe role conflict in this situation of value change.

The possibilities of role conflict for teachers in present cultural conditions are numerous. Teachers who hold 'traditional' values and who attempt to transmit them may find unexpected resistance and even ridicule from senior pupils towards these values. Teachers who hold 'emergent' values may find themselves in conflict with the expectations of the head teacher, their colleagues or the parents. Such situations may occur where there is a strong expectation that a teacher will have a specifically Christian religious and moral commitment, or they may occur over questions of professional values involving type of relationship with pupils or even appropriate dress.[22] Some teachers who are uncertain of their own values will be exposed to conflict if value certainty is expected of them by pupils or parents. The teacher in the working-class school may experience heightened value conflict as the already important culture gap between his own position and that of his pupils widens as the result of social change.

Musgrove and Taylor (1965) provide evidence that the moral orientation of the teacher's role is still strong. In their research, moral training was given greater weight than instruction in subjects, social training, education for family life, social advancement or education for citizenship by all teachers except male grammar-school teachers. King (1969), in his investigation of values in a grammar school, found that his teachers stressed the importance of honesty, truthfulness, tolerance and the 'traditional Christian values of behaviour and morality'. They were critical of mass media influences such as commercial television and particularly disapproved of the programme 'Double Your Money', reflecting, as King points out, their highly ranked belief 'that there is more to life than just material gratification'.[23] Such evidence suggests that many teachers will see their role as essentially in value conflict with wider cultural tendencies towards materialism, hedonism and relative rather than absolute moral standards, although the degree to which this is so and the various reactions of teachers to this situation remain largely unexplored.[24]

Conflict arising from the marginal role

Most role occupants like to feel that their activities are important and reasonably central to the institutions of which they are members and a conflict situation can arise when they perceive that they have only a marginal status so far as their colleagues or the management are concerned. Conflicts of marginal status can arise for teachers, as for other workers. Wilson illustrates this conflict with reference to the position of the teacher of humanities in a technical college where 'his subject is thought of—by colleagues and clientele alike—as a trimming, a piece of ministerial whitewash with no significance for the real business of the institution.'[25] In the past, where the emphasis of many secondary schools has been upon a narrow range of academic goals, the marginal status of teachers of certain subjects has been apparent. Teachers of art, woodwork and metalwork, technical and commercial studies, domestic science and physical education have had to face problems of this type, stemming partly from a view of their activities as 'extras' and partly, in the case of some of them, from a view of their role as 'instructors' rather than educators.

While the marginal status of many teachers of non-academic subjects has undoubtedly changed as a function of new organisational settings and a wider range of educational objectives, there is evidence that the problem has not entirely disappeared. Cannon (1964) has suggested that problems for the P.E. teacher in girls' grammar schools still exist and two studies have noted relatively high levels of role conflict and low levels of job satisfaction among teachers of domestic science (Rudd and Wiseman 1962; Musgrove 1967). Teachers of maths, science and foreign languages, on the other hand, appear to enjoy high status and security.

Marginal status is not necessarily always related to a particular teaching subject. The educational orientation of the head teacher and his 'patronage' of certain types of activity will be important determinants of teacher satisfaction and dissatisfaction in this area. If the head teacher's preferences are clearly visible in such matters as allocation of time and resources, selection of certain pupils for particular activities and publicity given to certain achievements, then marginal status role conflict can arise for teachers in a range of subjects. Widespread changes in educational goals can also create potential conflicts for teachers of subjects which have never been regarded as marginal in British secondary schools. The teacher of classics, for instance, has undergone in this century a radical change in the centrality of his role to the process of education, while the position of the teacher of technology has improved.

Teacher role conflict—the mediating variables

This chapter has outlined potential role conflict situations for the teacher. The extent to which teachers actually perceive these situations as problems or feel personally troubled by them will depend upon a considerable number of mediating variables. These are presented in the following schema:

a *Characteristics of the conflict* These will include the nature and intensity of the conflict and particularly, in the case of teachers, whether the issues involved relate to problems of 'moral orientation' or to 'self-orientation'.

b *Characteristics of the teacher* These will include age, sex, professional qualification and role concept (regarded as closely associated but not identical), subject specialism and age group specialism. Westwood, for instance, has suggested that role conflict exposure will be greatest for teachers in the middle of the professional hierarchy and least for those at the extremes—the infant school teacher and the university teacher. Important, also, will be the teacher's orientation to the conflict, his strategies of resolution and the general personality characteristics of the individual.

c *Characteristics of the school* These will include the characteristics of the head teacher, the way in which he conceives and performs his role, the goals set for the school, the size and organisation of the school, the characteristics of the clientele, the social class context and the relationships between the school and external agencies.

Such research as exists at present indicates that men teachers are more associated with conflict than women teachers (Getzels and Guba 1955), secondary modern school teachers than grammar-school teachers (Musgrove 1967) and teachers in working-class areas than their colleagues in middle-class areas (Taylor 1968). Some indications of the importance of the head teacher's role in relation to teacher conflict also exists and some evidence related to the influence of subject specialisms in the secondary school. The serious investigation of teacher role conflict however has hardly begun and very little is known about the incidence of various types of conflict or the extent to which particular groups of teachers are troubled by particular categories of role conflict.[26]

3 Present perspectives

The following chapters report the results of an investigation undertaken in the period 1967–70 into the intra-role conflicts of 150 secondary school teachers. The primary stimulus behind this work was the fact that Wilson's (1962) analysis of teacher role conflicts, which had suggested so many valuable lines of inquiry, remained virtually untested by empirical research, although the analysis itself was widely quoted in sociological studies in education.

The investigation had three major objectives. The first was to establish whether certain categories of role conflict suggested by Wilson were in fact seen as problem situations by a sample of serving teachers and, if so, how important these conflicts were thought to be in the teaching situation. An important related question was the extent to which the teachers as a whole had personally experienced such role conflicts as problems and had been to some degree troubled by them. A second objective was to investigate relationships between particular categories of teacher (classified by years of experience, professional qualification, sex, type of school, social composition of school and main subject specialism) and overall levels of perceived and experienced role conflict. The final major objective was to examine relationships between particular categories of teacher and particular categories of role conflict in order to reveal more precise 'role conflict profiles' than the initial measures would show.

The role conflict schedules* (first stage of inquiry)

To investigate both the perception and personal experience of role conflict by the sample, two schedules were devised, following a model outlined by Getzels and Guba (1955). Schedule I was designed to measure role conflict perception (RCP) and Schedule II to measure role conflict experience (RCE). The operational definition of role conflict used in the schedules was 'problems for the occupant which arise as the result of role incompatibilities'. The role conflict areas were therefore presented to the respondents as problems which teachers might meet with during the course of their work. Each area of role conflict was represented by two items which suggested role incompatibilities within the area. Four potential role conflict areas were presented: area I: Problems arising from role diffuseness; area II: Problems arising from role vulnerability; area III: Problems arising from tension between role commitment and career orientation; area IV: Problems arising from value conflicts.

A central problem arising from the diffuseness of the teacher's role (area I) was taken to be the difficulty of knowing what had been accomplished as the result of role performance. Thus the items in this area were concerned with knowledge or lack of knowledge of goal achievement as a factor in role conflict. This was expressed as follows, e.g. (item i) 'Whereas many occupations give clear "knowledge of results" to practitioners, teaching, by its very nature, can do this only to a limited extent.' The assumption in area I was that conflict could arise from this role ambiguity—from the incompatibility between the normal desire of role occupants to know what they were accomplishing and the relative invisibility of many of the teacher's achievements.[1]

In area II the concept of role vulnerability was introduced. The teacher's role was taken to be vulnerable and exposed to conflict in two senses. First, because the role, lacking the defences of mystique, jargon or narrowly defined technical expertise, could frequently be exposed to incompatible expectations from various external agencies, all of whom felt confident of their ability and right to define the teacher's role. This was expressed in (item iii) —'The teacher, unlike many professional practitioners, is subject

*Full details of the schedules are reported in Appendix I.

to a variety of conflicting opinions as to how he should carry out his professional work.' Second, vulnerability and hence conflict was seen to arise from the uncertain status of the teacher as a professional. This was expressed in (item iv)—'The teacher is a professional practitioner but despite this is generally treated as if he were not.' In this way, area II was designed to present role conflict arising from exposure to conflicting expectation and to conflicting perceptions of the professional role, seen as two related aspects of role vulnerability.[2]

Area III represented conflict between role commitment and career orientation. This was presented to the respondent in the following way, e.g. (item v)—'To obtain promotion, the teacher must be mobile and "gain experience", yet the nature of the work ideally requires a sustained relationship with particular groups of pupils.' The conflict suggested in this area was that between the widely held belief that promotion went to the 'movers' and the widely held belief that teachers should show loyalty to a school and its pupils.

The final area of role conflict focused upon incompatibility between the values which teachers were expected to uphold to the pupils and those which were generally current in society. This was expressed in—e.g. (item vii)—'The teacher is expected to maintain traditional values and standards yet at the same time society in general largely ignores these values and standards.'[3]

On schedule I, which was designed to measure role conflict perception, the teachers were asked to respond to each item on the following scale:

THIS SEEMS TO ME TO BE
- 0. Not a problem at all
- 1. A problem of little importance
- 2. A problem of moderate importance
- 3. A problem of great importance
- 4. A problem of very great importance

On schedule II, concerned with role conflict experience, the items of the first schedule were repeated but the teachers were asked to respond on a different scale:

I HAVE PERSONALLY FELT THIS AS A PROBLEM
- 0. Not at all
- 1. To a small extent

2. To a moderate extent
3. To a great extent
4. To a very great extent

Each respondent completed, in addition to the two schedules, a short personal questionnaire to elicit characteristics (years of experience, etc.) to be related to role conflict perception and experience.

It was felt that the best method of distributing the schedules was in group meetings with the teachers. The purpose here was threefold. In the first place, it gave an opportunity to the researcher to stress the distinction which was being made between perceived and experienced problems. Second, it gave an opportunity for the teachers to raise any queries regarding the schedules and to ask for any clarification. Finally, it made possible discussion in general terms of the value and purpose of the research.[4] The schedules were distributed at meetings in morning, midday or afternoon break periods, which were attended by most of the full-time staff of the schools approached. At these meetings, the teachers were asked to complete the schedules individually and not to discuss the issues arising until they had all made their responses. This they agreed to do. Completed schedules were handed in to the school secretaries (with the head teacher's permission) and collected at the school after one week.

In analysing the schedules, the distribution of scores over the whole range was first examined for each area of role conflict, with particular reference to the percentage of teachers scoring o to indicate rejection of the area as an actual problem (schedule I) or to indicate total lack of personal experience of the conflict (schedule II). The basic question of whether the suggested conflicts were meaningful in the teaching situation was involved in this analysis. Thereafter, for the purposes of comparison and evaluation between various groups of teachers and various areas of role conflict, scores were dichotomised on a low–high classification and the chi-square test applied to determine the significance of differences.[5]

In addition to analysis of scores in each role conflict area, the sum of scores on each schedule was taken as a measure of overall role conflict perception and overall role conflict experience for each respondent. Overall RCP and RCE scores were also dichotomised and compared by chi-square.[6] Comparison groups were formed using the variables of years of teaching experience, professional qualification, sex, type of school, main subject specialism[7] and social class composition of the schools.[8] For the latter, the following classification was used (see Taylor 1968)— schools where over 50 per cent of the pupils' fathers were in white-collar employment were regarded as 'middle-class'. Schools where the proportion of pupils from white-collar and manual working-class backgrounds were approximately equal were regarded as 'mixed'. Schools where the majority of the pupils' fathers were in manual employment were regarded as 'working-class'.

The interviews (second stage of inquiry)

Merton has suggested that the impersonal and limited nature of questionnaires as instruments of social research makes it necessary to use, where possible, interviews in order to explore the thinking, nuances and qualifications which lie behind the objective responses. This procedure was followed. The schedules, even though they provided considerable space for additional comment, could not be regarded as sufficient in themselves. While they revealed the broad outline of teacher reaction to suggested role conflict and indicated some valuable pointers towards explaining such reaction, they remained essentially surface instruments. To attempt to probe more deeply, a series of one-hour 'focused interviews'[9] was subsequently undertaken with 80 of the original 150 teachers.[10]

It was considered important also to interview the head teachers of the ten secondary schools which were involved, in order to obtain more information about the schools as organisations. Information regarding school 'climate', internal organisation and clientele was already available, partly from the researcher's own local knowledge of the schools,[11] and partly from the comments volunteered by the teachers during the interviews. The teachers had also, during the course of interviews, frequently made reference to the role of the head teacher as they perceived it in their various schools. One-hour focused interviews with the ten head teachers provided further useful information on how the heads conceived of their role in relation to the problem areas under investigation.

The sample and the sample area

The social context of the investigation was a prosperous Midland borough of approximately sixty thousand inhabitants. The town had developed particularly in the nineteenth century as the result of railway development and today it possesses important mechanical and electrical engineering industries. An above-average proportion of the male working population is composed of white-collar and skilled manual workers employed in industrial, technical and scientific activities. A considerable number of men are also employed outside the town in the car factories of a large Midland city. The standard of housing is generally good and there are few areas in the town which could be described as industrial slums. Some of the Victorian terraces in the central railway area of the town are occupied by West Indian and Indian families which together represent about 5 per cent of the total population.

The town has a public school and ten secondary schools, including two grammar schools, two bilateral schools[12] and six non-selective schools.[13] The boys' grammar school (voluntary aided) was founded in the late nineteenth century and provides places for about 600 pupils. It enjoys high status locally, arising partly from its association and scholarship connections with the public school. The girls' grammar school, which was founded in the early part of this century, provides places for a similar number of pupils. The two bilateral schools are also single sex and occupy modern buildings in a pleasant residential part of the town. Each school accommodates about 700 pupils. Of the six non-selective schools, one is a Roman Catholic foundation of 450 pupils (co-educational) and one a Church of England foundation of about 600 pupils (co-educational). The remaining schools vary between 300 and 400 pupils, two being co-educational and two single sex. The majority of the schools are in modern buildings and pleasant surroundings.

The total number of full-time secondary-school teachers (excluding head teachers and deputy head teachers) at the time of the inquiry was 223. Schedules were distributed to each one and 158 were returned, of which 150 were usable. The sample of 150 teachers consisted of 87 men and 63 women. 43 were grammar-school teachers (23 men and 20 women); 38 were bilateral-school teachers (25 men and 13 women); and 69 were secondary modern teachers (39 men and 30 women). The characteristics of the sample were compared with the characteristics of the total secondary-school teaching population in maintained schools in England and Wales as at March 1967.[14] This showed that the sample was very representative of the total secondary teaching population in respect of age structure and type of school, although it contained a somewhat higher proportion of younger teachers than was the case nationally. The sample was most atypical in the area of professional qualification, where graduate teachers were over-represented and certificated teachers under-represented in terms of their proportions in the national population.

The possibility of generalising the results of the inquiry beyond its immediate social context must be approached with some caution. While the sample of teachers studied was quite representative of the larger teaching population, the context within which they perform their roles was essentially 'small town' and 'small school'. Investigations in a metropolitan area, with more social problems and with larger secondary schools, would be likely to produce a different picture of role conflict in the teaching situation from that revealed in the following chapters.

4 Perceptions and experiences

It was apparent from the analysis of response to the four suggested role conflict areas on schedule I (area I—diffuse role; area II—role vulnerability; area III—role commitment *v*. career; area IV—value conflicts) that they were accepted by the sample as actual problem and conflict situations which teachers met with in their work. The percentage of respondents in each role conflict area scoring o to indicate 'no problem at all' was very small (I—4.7%; II—4.7%; III—2.7%; IV—5.3%). While all four role conflicts were in this way perceived as valid for teachers, some were clearly seen to be of greater importance than others.

TABLE I *Perceived importance of role conflicts* (n = 150)

Conflict area	% scoring	
	High	Low
Role commitment *v*. career orientation	64	36
Divergent value orientations	63.3	36.7
Role vulnerability	47.3	52.7
Role diffuseness	35.3	64.7

As Table I shows, conflicts between role commitment and career orientation and conflicts between divergent value orientations were regarded as problems of great importance in the teaching situation—almost two-thirds of the sample having high scores in these areas. Both these conflicts may be described in terms of 'moral orientation' since they have to do with ethical and value considerations. The conflicts of role vulnerability and role diffuseness on the other hand may be described in terms of 'self orientation' since they have to do with the individual's perceptions, satisfactions and self concept. It is characteristic of the historical background and tradition of the teaching profession that the teachers as a whole should see conflicts of moral orientation as of greater importance than conflicts of self orientation.

This concern with values and the conflicts between felt commitment to pupils and the perceived realities of promotion and advancement in teaching was further revealed during the course of the interviews and this material is commented upon in detail later (see chapters 7 and 8). While there were important differences in teacher response to these role conflicts, statements such as the following catch the spirit of many of the reactions:

(*Values*)
'It's largely our job to maintain values—teaching is about values.' (Man graduate: age 62: grammar)

'Today's teenagers seem to be becoming "conditioned" against traditional standards and it is increasingly difficult for the teacher to impress upon them the value of such standards.' (Woman certificated: age 26: s. modern)

'It is the teacher's business to uphold traditional standards— if the teacher doesn't, who does? A lot of parents aren't worried.' (Man certificated: age 37: s. modern)

'The thing that worries me is dishonesty—it seems to me to have increased and the attitude to it has changed. Generally, honesty is no longer thought important.' (Woman certificated: age 54: bilateral)

(*Commitment v. career*)
'Should one be loyal to one's students and give them continuity, or go glory- and cash-chasing around the country?' (Man certificated: age 53: s. modern)

'The people responsible for promoting teachers to headships equate "experience" with moving from school to school instead of from pupil to pupil; viz. person-centred teaching.' (Man graduate: age 34: bilateral)

'Staff are forced to move from school to school in order to obtain promotion—promotions are rarely made within a school. This is a big fault in the system.' (Woman certificated: age 27: s. modern)

'I've been asked—"Why did you stay in that school for five years?" Interviewing boards look for width of experience. It depends which you put first—your own career or educating the pupils.' (Man graduate: age 48: bilateral)

The analysis of schedule I revealed that the teachers perceived role conflicts in the four areas and rated as particularly important conflicts of 'moral orientation', but it gave no indication of the extent of personal experience of these conflicts. This was revealed in schedule II.

The percentage of respondents scoring 0 on this schedule, to indicate that they had personally felt each conflict 'not at all', was, as expected, markedly higher than on schedule I. 22.7 per cent (34) of the teachers claimed to have had no personal experience of conflict between role commitment and career orientation (19 women : 15 men). 16.7 per cent (25) had not been troubled at all by conflicts of role vulnerability (13 grammar : 12 others) and 13.3 per cent (20) had no experience of troubling value conflicts in their teaching role (13 men : 7 women). Of the 11.3 per cent (17) who scored 0 in the role diffuseness area, 12 were graduates and 5 certificated teachers.

The majority had however some personal and troubling experience of each of the role conflicts, although the overall level of scores was low compared with schedule I. The lower level of role conflict experience shown in Table 2 was to be expected since the teachers had been asked to make a clear distinction between perceptions and experiences. Differences between the scores in Table 1 and Table 2 are obviously affected by such variables as age, sex, professional qualification, type of school and type of teaching within a school. While grammar-school teachers, for instance, *saw* an important conflict situation in the area of values, their personal experience of this conflict could be expected

TABLE 2 *Extent of personal experience of role conflict* (n = 150)

Conflict area	% scoring	
	High	Low
Divergent value orientations	36	64
Role diffuseness		
Role commitment *v.* career orientation	26	74
Role vulnerability	22	78

to be at a much lower level than that of secondary modern teachers. Similarly, while women teachers generally accepted that there was an important conflict between role commitment and career orientation in teaching, their own personal experience of such conflict was expected to be at a lower level than that of men teachers. The influence of personality factors is also important. Kahn and his co-authors (1964, pp. 223-333) found that several personality dimensions mediated significantly the degree to which perceived conflict was experienced as strain by the focal person. These dimensions included emotional sensitivity, introversion/extroversion, flexibility/rigidity and the need for career achievement.

Schedule II, with its focus upon direct personal experience of role conflict, naturally discriminated more sharply between various categories of teacher than had schedule I. Further analysis was to show that some categories of teacher had hardly any personal experience of role conflicts which had troubled some of their colleagues to a high degree. While allowing for these differences, the emergence of value conflict as the most important area of role conflict experience for the sample as a whole is yet further evidence of the concern which many teachers have for this sector of their role.

Categories of teacher and levels of role conflict

The sum of scores in the four areas on each schedule was taken as a measure of overall role conflict. These scores were dichotomised and the results compared by chi-square. The purpose here was to reveal relationships between various groups of teachers and overall levels of conflict broadly defined in terms of 'low' and 'high'.

Categories of teacher associated with significantly higher levels of role conflict perception,[1] measured and defined in this way, were teachers of more than ten years experience (56.7 per cent score high compared with 34.9 per cent of teachers with less than ten years experience: $p < 0.01$); certificated teachers (55.7 per cent score high compared with 35 per cent of graduates: $p < 0.02$); secondary modern teachers (56.5 per cent score high compared with 34.9 per cent of grammar-school teachers and 34.2 per cent of bilateral school teachers: $p < 0.05$); men secondary modern teachers (66.7 per cent score high compared with 35.4 per cent of other men teachers: $p < 0.01$).

Analysis of overall role conflict experience (RCE) largely reinforced the relationship shown by schedule I, but significant differences in the scores of men and women teachers and of teachers in schools of varying social class composition now become apparent.

Categories of teacher associated with significantly higher levels of overall role conflict experience[2] were men teachers (24.1 per cent score high compared with 4.7 per cent of women teachers: $p < 0.01$); certificated teachers (24.3 per cent score high compared with 8.8 per cent of graduates: $p < 0.01$); secondary modern teachers (26.1 per cent score high compared with 2.3 per cent of grammar-school teachers: $p < 0.01$); men secondary modern teachers (38.5 per cent score high compared with 12.5 per cent of other men teachers: $p < 0.02$) and teachers in 'working-class' schools (27.3 per cent score high compared with 2.3 per cent of teachers in 'middle-class' schools: $p < 0.01$).

Experienced teachers

The significantly higher perception of role conflict by the more experienced teachers was to be expected in terms of length of exposure to problem situations in teaching. It can be argued from the findings of this study that the longer a teacher serves the more likely he is to perceive high levels of role conflict.[3] This argument, however, cannot be made in the case of role conflict experience, where no significant differences were apparent between more and less experienced teachers.[4] It seems probable that while perception of conflict increases, teachers who remain in the profession over time adapt themselves so that personal concern about these conflicts is kept to a comparatively low level. This is clearly a necessary process for occupational survival.[5] Some of the adaptations will probably involve such 'functional' characteristics as greater confidence and stability, a wider professional perspective and a repertoire of strategies and techniques for dealing with the problem situations of teaching. 'Dysfunctional' adaptations may take the form of a reduction of identification with the teaching role, the abandonment of certain goals and ideals or the development of a cynical and hard-bitten attitude to educational matters.

Certificated and graduate

The fact that certificated teachers perceived and experienced significantly more conflict than graduate teachers raised some interesting questions. Since over 50 per cent of the graduates were in schools other than grammar and over 25 per cent of the certificated teachers were in schools other than secondary modern, this finding could not be interpreted simply as another aspect of the expected differences between grammar and secondary modern schools. The possibility had to be considered that graduates, within all types of school, might define their role in narrower terms than certificated teachers and might in addition feel more confident of their status as teachers, thus making them less exposed to role conflict. Analysis within schools showed that graduate teachers were less likely than certificated teachers to perceive high levels of role conflict in bilateral and secondary modern schools, although numbers were small and differences did not reach statistical significance.[6] There is nevertheless some tentative indication that a teacher's professional qualification does mediate role conflict in a school situation. The Certificate in Education as a professional qualification and the concept of the teacher's role formed within the college of education environment seem to expose certificated teachers to conflict, particularly in the role vulnerability and role diffuseness areas.[7]

School type

The secondary modern school emerged as a more conflict-prone environment than either the grammar school or the bilateral school. Teachers in such schools perceived significantly more conflict than did their colleagues in other schools and their personal experience of troubling conflict was at a much higher level than that of their grammar school colleagues.

So far as perceived role conflict is concerned, this finding confirms that of Musgrove (1967) who also found higher levels of conflict among secondary modern school teachers than among grammar school teachers. Analysis within each area of role conflict was to show that while problems of goal attainment, role commitment and divergent values were important for secondary modern school teachers, their high scores in the role vulnerability area particularly marked them out from their grammar and bilateral school colleagues.[8]

Men and women

Men teachers, as earlier studies had shown, were more associated with high levels of role conflict than were women teachers. This was particularly true of role conflict experience and the pattern was most apparent in the case of men teachers in secondary modern schools. Here, the overall RCE scores of men teachers were significantly higher than those of women teachers, with 38.5 per cent of the men scoring high compared with 10 per cent of the women (p <0.02).

Clearly, men teachers were likely to have had much more experience of conflict in area III (role commitment *v.* career orientation) and a good deal of the variance in the scores of men and women teachers can be accounted for by this sex-specific factor. Even allowing for this, however, interesting and important differences occurred in relation to other role conflicts, particularly area I (role diffuseness) and area II (role vulnerability) suggesting that men teachers were more sensitive to these as problems.[9] Getzels and Guba (1955, p. 37), in reporting significantly higher scores for men teachers in comparison with women teachers, commented:

since teaching is often thought of as a woman's profession it is not surprising to find that men should be more liable to the conflicts in the teaching situation than women. For women, teaching is a respected occupation often representing a top level vocational goal. They can be more tolerant of the inconsistencies in expectations since it is not likely that they could do better professionally elsewhere.

This suggestion of a higher level of tolerance by women of inconsistencies in teaching receives further support from this study. During the course of interviews women teachers, while recognising the existence of certain incompatibilities in the teaching situation, generally maintained a tolerant attitude towards them. These interviews involved few of the expressions of annoyance, suggestions for reform or detailed criticisms which emanated from the men.

The higher scores of the men may also be associated with higher levels of achievement orientation and with greater identification with the teaching role. Kahn *et al.* (1964, p. 384) have pointed out that 'an individual who is strongly achievement oriented exhibits a high degree of personal involvement with his job and the adverse effects of role conflict are more pronounced for him than for those who are less involved.' It is only possible to speculate here since no measures of achievement orientation or role identification were used, but it may well be that the higher level of role conflict experience for men is related to a more intense achievement orientation and a closer identification with the teaching role than that which characterises their women colleagues.[10]

Men teachers in secondary modern schools

Within the male teaching group and within the sample of teachers as a whole, men teachers in secondary modern schools emerged as being particularly prone to high levels of role conflict perception and to relatively high levels of role conflict experience. 66.7 per cent of men teachers in such schools had high RCP scores compared with 35.4 per cent of men teachers in other secondary schools (p < 0.01). This difference held for role conflict experience, where 38.5 per cent of secondary modern men had high scores compared with only 12.5 per cent of other men teachers (p <0.01). Detailed consideration of these differences will be made in subsequent chapters but at this point the particular exposure of men secondary modern school teachers to role conflict requires comment.

Such exposure could be logically predicted from the relationships already suggested between various characteristics of teachers and exposure to role conflict. In this case, a general tendency for men teachers to score more highly than women teachers is reinforced by two other conflict related factors—performance of the teaching role within a secondary modern school and possession of certificated rather than graduate status.[11] Hargreaves (1967) noted that many of the men teachers in the secondary modern schools which he studied were ambivalent about their jobs and tended to take a pessimistic view of the outcome of their work. In the short interviews of the present study, such characteristics were not generally apparent but this group of teachers was clearly concerned about problems of goal attainment, role vulnerability, conflict of commitment and career and value discontinuities which they faced and such concern could be productive of pessimism over time.

Role conflict and teacher expectation

A good deal of attention is being focused at present upon the importance of teacher expectation as a factor in pupils' performance and the suggestion has been made that many teachers take an unduly pessimistic view of the capabilities of their pupils.[12] While such expectations are obviously related to the concept of intelligence which teachers hold and to structural factors such as streaming, it is possible that a teacher's pessimism about his own role situation will have generalised effects upon his performance and upon his expectations of the pupils. Some evidence suggesting such a connection is available. Bacchus (1967, pp. 147-50), investigating the attitudes of men secondary modern teachers towards their pupils, found that those who were adversely critical of their pupils were much more anxious and pessimistic about their own status than were those teachers who took a more favourable view. Further investigation into the determinants of teacher expectations may reveal that a teacher's exposure to high levels of role conflict and the consequences of this situation are factors of some importance in effecting the climate of learning.

The social context

The social class composition of the ten schools involved in this inquiry was found to be an important variable related to teachers' role conflict experience. Of the ten schools, two were classified as 'middle class', three as 'socially mixed' and the remaining five as 'working class'. 27.3 per cent of the teachers in working-class schools had high RCE scores compared with 15.4 per cent in socially mixed schools and only 2.3 per cent in middle-class schools. The differences between the scores in working-class and middle-class schools were highly significant ($p < 0.01$).

It is a commonplace of sociological writings in education that the teacher of working-class pupils is faced with a potentially more intense role conflict situation than teachers in schools of other social class compositions. That this is in fact the case has been shown by Becker (1952a) and Herriott and St John (1966) in America, and by Taylor (1968) in Britain. The results of the present study give further evidence of this relationship and follow-up interviews with teachers in such schools indicated that conflicts and ambiguities related to goal attainment and to value questions were particularly important in this connection.

This chapter has shown that the conflicts arising from role diffuseness, role vulnerability, role commitment v. career orientation and role value orientation were seen to be actual problems of the teaching situation and that conflicts of 'moral orientation' were rated as particularly important by the sample of teachers. Dr Bryan Wilson's suggestion (1962, pp. 30-1) that teachers face 'a most significant role conflict arising from the divergence of role commitment and career orientation' was supported by the findings, and also his arguments concerning 'the conflict of a role which implies specific value commitments, performed in a society where these values are at best only partially supported'. Distinctions have however been established between the perception of role conflicts in the teaching situation and personal experience of such conflicts and the importance of mediating variables such as age, sex, professional qualification and type of school has been demonstrated.

It is necessary now to examine more closely the relationships between particular groups of teachers and particular role conflicts, using interview material to give some deeper insights.

5   Diffuseness and conflict

When Lawrence wrote of his teaching experience—'you never know what you have done or if you really have done anything'— he clearly felt the diffuseness and ambiguity of the teacher's role to be a problem. In so far as the teacher's concern goes beyond measurable levels of knowledge and skill to include some influence upon the pupil's sensitivity, appreciation, interests, attitudes and values, then the role has a diffuse commitment. This diffuseness may create conflict or ambiguity for those who wish or need to know if they are accomplishing anything in these areas but cannot, for a number of reasons, have any firm knowledge of this. On the other hand, it can be argued that teachers receive many indications and signs as to the more widespread effects of their work and that only neurotics such as Lawrence would regard diffuseness as a problem in itself.

The teachers as a whole, in this study, saw conflict associated with role diffuseness as the least significant of the four conflicts suggested to them. However, such conflict was not dismissed completely. Over one-third of the teachers rated it as of high importance in the teaching situation and approximately one in four had been personally troubled to a considerable degree by such conflict. Table 3 shows the percentage of teachers from each comparison group with high scores on perceived or experienced role conflict in this area.

Significant differences were apparent between more experienced and less experienced teachers in the perception of this conflict and secondary modern teachers had significantly higher levels of

TABLE 3   *RCP and RCE: % of high scores in the role diffuseness area[a]*

	RCP	RCE
(87) Men	40.2	31.0
(63) Women	28.6	19.0
(83) Teachers[b]	27.7	25.3
(67) Teachers[c]	44.8[d]	26.9
(69) S. modern	43.5	34.4[d]
(43) Grammar	27.9	13.9
(69) S. modern	43.5	34.4
(38) Bilateral	28.9	23.7
(39) Men s. modern	53.8[d]	38.5
(48) Other men	29.2	25.0
(30) Women s. modern	30.0	30.0
(33) Other women	27.3	9.1

[a]No significant differences were found between the scores of grammar and bilateral school teachers.
[b]Less than 10 years experience.
[c]More than 10 years experience.
[d]Significant differences in χ^2 test beyond the 5 % level.

conflict experience than their grammar-school colleagues. While men teachers in secondary modern schools had significantly higher perception scores than other men teachers, an interesting general tendency for men to score more highly than women, both in secondary modern and grammar schools, also emerged. 53.8 per cent of men teaching in secondary modern schools saw conflicts of role diffuseness as highly important, compared with 30 per cent of women teaching in such schools ($p < 0.05$). 43.5 per cent of men teaching in grammar schools had high scores in this area compared with only 10 per cent of women grammar-school teachers ($p < 0.05$). That these findings did not hold for the bilateral schools seems to be a result of specific situational factors.[1]

The analysis of the role conflict schedules showed that men teachers, experienced teachers and secondary modern school teachers were more associated with conflicts of role diffuseness than were their colleagues. While it was possible to speculate about reasons for this situation, it seemed desirable that the teachers themselves should explain as far as possible their various reactions to this conflict and the interviews were undertaken with this objective. The interviews helped to clarify further the associations already revealed by the schedules but they provided also an indication of the complexity of the relationships and demonstrated that the schedules had revealed tendencies to which there were interesting exceptions.

The interviews

During the course of the interviews, three broad patterns of reaction became apparent. The minority of high scorers agreed with Lawrence that there was an important problem in knowing what you had accomplished in teaching. Their replies revealed the importance of type of school, nature of teaching subject, the role concept of the teacher and the influence of personality factors in making for exposure to this particular type of conflict:

'Some of us need to know that we are successful in what we do. This is your own need to believe that you are succeeding. There is no way of knowing your success in English as there is in Maths. I aim to get them to perceive relationships—to become aware—this can't be measured by exams. It depends on your own faith in yourself—some are certain that they are doing well—I'm not yet certain. Perhaps we need to be accepted as successful by other people.' (Man certificated: age 46: s. modern)

'In order to retain one's dream, it's terribly helpful to be able to see or appear to see results—to meet former pupils. This is more difficult in secondary modern than in primary or grammar schools. To see that some of one's pupils have made successes or express gratitude, gives one confidence and hope for the future, in a profession where many people seem to be lacking in a hopeful attitude especially in the secondary modern situation. The teacher has to have faith in what he is doing. Many teachers lose their faith, like priests who have lost their vocation.' (Man certificated: age 54: s. modern)

49

'I frankly have felt that this was one of the most disturbing and frustrating aspects of teaching—because one couldn't be very sure of what one had accomplished. My outlook may be conditioned by being a teacher of R.E. One is conscious of resistance to the subject, and among the older age groups, resentment. This can give rise to cynicism on the part of the teacher.' (Man certificated: age 59: s. modern)

'One never has a very clear picture of what one has done—sometimes I have the feeling that the pupils would have passed the exams without my efforts.

In education, you are working in the dark for a future generation. I am doubtful about my influence on a broader scale—if the general standards in society are a sign, then we are failing.' (Man certificated: age 46: s. modern)

'The teacher can never know what she has really accomplished. This does worry me to a very great extent. Teachers go forward in faith—you surmise that things are going in—you can never judge.' (Woman certificated: age 36: s. modern)

'I have felt more conscious of this in recent years as a result of getting older—you look back over twenty years—you question it more—what has been accomplished? Teaching History—the information doesn't stick—the attitude and way of thinking is the important thing—this is where one has very little certainty of achievement.' (Man graduate: age 50: grammar)

Teachers who saw an important problem situation in this area stressed different aspects of diffuseness in the teacher's role. Some held very broad concepts of the role and as a consequence felt more exposed to uncertainties related to goal achievement. As one teacher put it:

The teacher in the examination system has a measure of his results. Being more concerned with education for living, other teachers will always be in some doubt as to the effect of their work—it's a situation comparable to the work of the priest.

It is a problem because we want to know how effective and useful we are—it's not a power complex. We want to be as effective as possible for the child.

Teachers in this category were generally concerned about the moral and social aspects of their role as well as the academic aspects. Other teachers discussed diffuseness in more subject-related terms. In so far as they looked beyond knowledge for signs of sensitivity, critical awareness and genuine response, some of them met with a feeling of uncertainty. The secondary modern school provided the context within which most of these teachers encountered problems of diffuseness. Similar reactions in other types of school were exceptional.

The majority who saw this role conflict as of little significance and who felt relatively untroubled by it, divided into two groups. By far the largest group felt that the teacher could and did know the results of his work in various ways, or they accepted that problems of goal attainment existed in schools other than their own. A smaller group accepted that there was intangibility but they regarded this as an inevitable characteristic of the teacher's work.

Among those who saw 'results', considerable stress was placed upon meeting former pupils as being a source of satisfaction and feedback for the teacher, if the teacher stayed long enough in the community to make this possible:

'If he remains at the job, he regularly meets old scholars. They are a very good indication as to the results of his work. You *do* know—provided you're there to know. You've lived—you've been there—you've had an effect. Your life in a community has been effective.' (Man certificated: age 50: s. modern)

'The successful pupils come back to see you—this is very rewarding. You have made a contact with the child, some kind of impression.' (Woman certificated: age 57: bilateral)

'In later years, we find many of the less academically able boys have blossomed out into excellent leaders of society, with a clear sense of gratitude for the teaching they received at school.' (Man graduate: age 63: grammar)

Examination results were another important indicator. Teachers in secondary modern schools who referred to examinations as a measure of what they had accomplished, generally commented that education involved more than examination passing, but they frankly admitted that examination results gave considerable satisfaction and a sense of achievement both to the pupil and to the teacher:

'I feel I'm doing the wrong thing in pushing for the examination and yet I know it is important. The examination results give me a lot of satisfaction—a sign that I haven't wasted my time.' (Man certificated: age 36: s. modern)

'External exams help to keep me going—I see something of what I have done.' (Woman certificated: age 36: s. modern)

Teachers in other secondary schools tended to accept examinations as natural facts of educational life and as important evidence of a teacher's work. There were indications also that some of them held specific rather than diffuse role concepts with consequently less exposure to role ambiguity:

'Results in "O" levels are a measure—the ticket to the career is important for boys and for the teacher. There is satisfaction in helping boys on the career road.' (Man graduate: age 35: bilateral)

'You do get some feedback—I feel that I've done what I'm expected to do. I look on it in terms of limited objectives—"O" level passes. You set yourself an objective and you try to achieve it—goals are important.' (Man certificated: age 28: bilateral)

'Given the type of school that I am at, exams dominate the curriculum. I do see results in GCE—most go to university afterwards. I look at it from a subject point of view. Basically what I'm there for is to look after them so far as French is concerned.' (Man graduate: age 40: grammar)

'My attitude is primarily that of a scientist—primarily my objective is to get them to think scientifically—to teach them to use their brains. I think there is an awful lot of nonsense talked about influencing character.' (Man graduate: age 36: grammar)

Some of the teachers in bilateral and grammar schools felt that they were protected from diffuse role conflict because of the specific characteristics of the schools in which they worked:

'This problem differs according to type of school. One geared to an examination programme does not face this sort of problem.' (Man graduate: age 40: bilateral)

'I would think this is more of a problem in the non-selective schools. In the selectives you do see—with the examination results and the general attitude of the children.' (Woman graduate: age 54: grammar)

Considerable stress was placed by teachers in all types of school upon the importance of pupil response and interest in providing a valuable sign to the teacher of what he was accomplishing. There were references to the teacher 'knowing this intuitively', sensing it and feeling it. Work with the sixth form was obviously an important source of satisfaction in this connection, providing a sense of culmination and achievement:

'There *is* very considerable feedback—you know it by the same token as you know a person's on your wavelength. It's a thing you sense—interest and response are demonstrated in relationships.' (Man graduate: age 32: bilateral)

'It may be just relevant to me as an art teacher—the main result I look for is that the boys enjoy the lesson. I'm not interested in beautiful paintings produced. Exam results mean nothing. I get a good response from the boys.' (Man certificated: age 28: s. modern)

'There *are* very strong indications of what you have accomplished. In my personal experience—the girls respond so much—you can see whether you are achieving something. It's important to get them to think for themselves—to be able to argue. You can see this at the "A" level stage—it's very satisfying. To see their development at this stage is fascinating.' (Woman graduate: age 25: grammar)

'The VIth form give colossal satisfaction—they repay all the despair which you feel with some of the others. With some classes you feel like a voice crying in the wilderness. It's *response* that gives satisfaction. I can't bear them not showing response—perhaps it's pride.' (Woman certificated: age 48: bilateral)

No statistically significant differences in this area of conflict emerged from comparisons of the scores of teachers in various subject groups, but there were interesting indications throughout that teaching subject had an effect. Mathematics teachers in particular were low scorers on problems of role diffuseness. A not uncommon view during the interviews was that expressed by a grammar-school teacher:

'I answered as a maths teacher—a maths teacher has a pretty good idea of what he has accomplished.'

It was apparent from the interviews that those teachers who rejected role diffuseness as a serious problem or conflict situation did so for a variety of reasons. The unifying characteristic of the group was however the fact that they all saw satisfying feedback of the results of their efforts. In this feedback, contact with former pupils, examination results, work with the sixth form and evidence of pupil responsiveness were important components.

A small group of teachers, while agreeing that there was no serious conflict related to role diffuseness, took a definably different approach. Essentially, their view was, that intangibility and diffuseness was an inevitable and accepted part of the teacher's role performance. The emphasis of their replies was that the teacher did not expect to know what he had accomplished, but the important thing was to do the job conscientiously and that the teacher could not and should not become preoccupied with the question of results. While both men and women made such a response it was a point of view more associated during the interviews with women teachers than with men teachers:

'This is an accepted fact, not a problem—it is inherent in any work of a similar nature, e.g. that of a clergyman. One teaches Art or Music or Poetry in the knowledge that you will rarely reach all your audience but that however few you inspire it is worth doing.' (Woman graduate: age 53: grammar)

'I don't see this as a problem. The influence you have over your pupils you can never see—the results may be very long term. You do your best—you don't expect to know.' (Woman graduate: age 54: bilateral)

'Not a great worry or a great problem. What one accomplishes varies from group to group. If you are concerned about the individuals in a group and you are conscientiously trying to give of your best—then you can't worry about it.' (Woman certificated: age 49: s. modern)

'So much of teaching involves intangibles that one cannot rightly seek "knowledge of results" except in the area of factual learning, i.e. in one part only of the whole range of the teacher's activity.' (Man graduate: age 32: bilateral)

Role conflict and educational change

The majority of secondary school teachers in this study were relatively untroubled by conflicts arising from role diffuseness, particularly if they were teaching in grammar or bilateral schools. However, there were indications that this situation might alter as the result of various changes taking place in education.

During the interviews the teachers were asked how changes in education (generally in relation to their main subject) were affecting their role and particularly their sense of goal achievement. Some of the teachers had been closely involved in an ambitious inter-disciplinary project in one of the schools and other teachers were involved in developing new approaches to teaching and learning, ranging from 'new' maths and Nuffield science and French to co-operation in projects sponsored by the local and active Teachers' Centre. There was plenty of evidence that these teachers had found a higher level of interest among their pupils as a result of these approaches but there was also evidence of some concern over what had been accomplished in actual learning. It can be argued that the move from conventional teacher-directed and subject-centred activity to largely pupil-centred activity involves an increase in the diffuseness of the teacher's role. In many of these new developments the teacher no longer mediates specific and predetermined knowledge to the pupils, but undertakes a more open, organisational role in creating the conditions for learning and understanding to take place. The move to open learning situations sometimes involves a teacher in becoming a member of a teaching team or in co-operating in projects which cut across traditional subject specialisms. For some teachers this involves a radical reorientation of their role in the direction of greater diffuseness and this has consequences for their experience of role conflict.[2] There was evidence that this was happening during the transition between the old role concept and the new role concept:

'When you have a class all to yourself—you bring them up in your way. Something is missing in IDS—particularly in first year. They are not your children in the open situation.' (Woman certificated: age 57: bilateral)

'IDS is less tangible in measuring how much you think *you've* done—the teacher as opposed to the children. In terms of interest and attitudes it is better.' (Man graduate: age 34: bilateral)

'It's easier with the traditional maths to know what you've accomplished. With modern maths, we are just now getting a standard—before that, it was difficult to know where we were going.' (Woman graduate: age 35: bilateral)

'Nuffield Science is not a success—it doesn't work with our pupils. It's less satisfying—attempting to do too many things at once. At the end of two years of Nuffield work there was no sense of having accomplished anything in terms of scientific knowledge—this is playing at science rather than getting down to solid learning.' (Man certificated: age 29: s. modern)

'Modern maths is more a matter of stimulating interest but you see less knowledge result in the new method. It is more difficult to teach—you don't see the end product so easily.' (Woman graduate: age 38: grammar)

While some teachers felt an increase in diffuseness as a result of new methods, others stressed the gain in pupil responsiveness and understanding and therefore of a sense of greater achievement. As one teacher put it:

'In modern maths you know much more what you have accomplished. In traditional maths you don't—they perform tricks.'

No objective measures of responses to educational change were taken and quantification could be based only upon content analysis of the interviews. This revealed that of the twenty-seven teachers interviewed who had been associated with such new developments, eighteen referred to the problem of knowing what had been accomplished, nine referred to a greater sense of achievement, while nearly all claimed that there had been an increase in pupil interest. Clearly such small numbers do not permit any firm conclusions about the relationships between changing concepts of the teacher's role and exposure to conflict associated with role diffuseness, but they do suggest that further research into the nature of these relationships would be worthwhile.

Role conflict and organisational change

Teachers in secondary schools are not only exposed at present to developments which radically change the nature of their role but they are also exposed to developments which radically change the context within which they perform these roles. Changes in the organisation and structure of schools have far-reaching implications for teacher role conflicts as Hoyle (1969) and Musgrove and Taylor (1969) have suggested.

The teachers in the present study had been unaffected as yet by comprehensive reorganisation but established teachers in the boys' grammar school had experienced over time changes in the size and social composition of the school. These changes were referred to by some of the teachers as having had an important effect upon teacher–pupil relationships, upon the teacher's sense of achievement and upon the whole ethos of the school:[3]

'When the school was smaller and one knew the boys personally it was so much easier to see the effect of one's work. As schools get bigger it is more difficult to know what you have accomplished, especially with boys in the lower streams—the personal element is lacking.'

'I have been in schools where there has been a very strong sense of community—the boys always came back. The modern trend is against this—you lose a lot of the boys—you never see them again—you cannot see so much of what you have accomplished in present day schools. It is the way society is developing— boys don't feel so attached.

The atmosphere of schools is changing—social influences have caused the boys to see the school as the place they come to, to get examination successes—and the sense of family is not what it used to be. The view of the master is of a person who is paid to get you through the exam. You feel that they are there, trying to get what they feel are their rights.'

It may be that the continued growth in the size of schools and possible loss of a feeling of community will affect the satisfactions of older teachers accustomed to close relationships with former pupils as an important part of their sense of achievement.[4]

Summary

Kahn *et al.* (1964), p. 94, in their investigation of role diffuseness or role ambiguity in industrial positions, found it to be 'a prevalent condition in organizational life', and at high levels of experience to be associated with feelings of strain and futility. The findings here are less dramatic. Conflict arising from role diffuseness or ambiguity was not a prevalent condition of the teaching situation in general, although men teachers, particularly if working in secondary modern schools, were prone to relatively high levels of conflict perception and experience. Higher levels of conflict associated with role diffuseness had been expected for secondary modern school teachers, but higher levels of conflict among men teachers in both secondary modern and grammar schools was unexpected. No firm indicators of why this should be emerged from the interviews. Possible reasons which have been suggested are that men identify more closely with the teaching role and as a result register higher levels of conflict or that men have a greater need to know what they have accomplished in role performance, a greater 'need for cognition' than women teachers.[5]

Also speculative must be the consideration of the consequences of high levels of unresolved conflict and ambiguity in this area. There was little evidence of feelings of strain and futility among the teachers. There was evidence of concern among the high scorers about problems of goal achievement and a desire for more recognition of a teacher's efforts by head teachers but a study in greater depth would be needed to probe emotional and other consequences. There were suggestions that knowledge of results helped to maintain a teacher's confidence and optimism especially in the secondary modern school and that lack of this knowledge contributed towards pessimism and cynicism.[6] One man, who had subsequently left teaching, commented: 'One of the most disturbing experiences of my time in teaching was the cynicism of the teachers—some pupils were unregenerate. The older teachers showed it most—perhaps it was the frustration of always teaching the slow pupil.' Whether this characteristic was a result of prolonged exposure to conflicts of diffuseness and ambiguity in the secondary modern school is a question in urgent need of further investigation.

6 Vulnerability and conflict

Frequently exposed to incompatible expectations about how and what they should teach, and struggling for professional status, teachers in America are generally seen to be in a vulnerable position, beset with conflict. This sample of British secondary-school teachers felt more secure in their professional status and less vulnerable to external pressures than is characteristically the case with American teachers. Less than half (47.3 per cent) saw conflicts of role vulnerability as of high importance in the teaching situation and less than one-quarter (22 per cent) had been personally troubled to any extent by such conflicts. Comparison of the scores of various categories of teacher, however, modified this general picture in important respects.

Teachers in secondary modern schools were once more differentiated from their colleagues by significantly higher scores. For the secondary modern teacher, conflicts of role vulnerability had a reality in terms of personal experience which hardly existed in grammar and bilateral schools. Grammar-school teachers in particular were hardly touched at all by personal experience of role vulnerability and the differences between the scores of these two categories of teacher were statistically very significant.

Role vulnerability on the conflict schedules was a composite area of exposure to conflicting expectations for the teaching role and exposure to conflicting evaluations of the teacher's professional status. Item (iii) had suggested that the teacher was vulnerable because he 'is subject to a variety of conflicting opinions as to how he should carry out his professional work'.

60

TABLE 4 *RCP and RCE: % of high scores in the role vulnerability area*[a]

	RCP	RCE
(87) Men	45.9	25.3
(63) Women	49.2	17.5
(83) Teachers[b]	44.6	16.9
(67) Teachers[c]	50.7	28.3
(69) S. modern	63.7[e]	36.2[e]
(43) Grammar	25.6	4.7
(69) S. modern	63.7[d]	36.2[d]
(38) Bilateral	42.1	15.8
(39) Men s. modern	64.1[e]	41.0[e]
(48) Other men	31.2	12.5
(30) Women s. modern	63.3[d]	30.0[d]
(33) Other women	36.4	6.1

[a]No significant differences were found between the scores of grammar and bilateral school teachers.
[b]Less than 10 years experience.
[c]More than 10 years experience.
[d]Significant differences in χ^2 test beyond the 5% level.
[e]Significant differences in χ^2 test beyond the 1% level.

Item (iv) had suggested vulnerability in relation to professional status—'The teacher is a professional practitioner but despite this is generally treated as if he were not.' Although inter-item correlation of scores was at an acceptable level, important qualitative differences in teacher reaction to these two suggested aspects of vulnerability were revealed during the interviews. For this reason, interview material for each item is presented separately.

Incompatible expectations

It can be argued that exposure to incompatible expectations for a role will not of itself create serious personal conflict for the role occupant, unless these expectations are accompanied by pressures to comply and by sanctions for non-compliance. Here an important distinction exists between the situations of the British and American teacher. While both may be subject to a variety of conflicting expectations for their role, the teacher in Britain, unlike his American counterpart, experiences very little pressure associated with these expectations. Consequently, he feels free to determine his own role concept and his own role behaviour in a situation of virtual autonomy.

This sense of freedom and autonomy emerged as the characteristic response of almost all the teachers interviewed:

'Opinions there may well be, of differing complexities, but the teacher is the sole arbiter of how he decides to do his job in the classroom.' (Man graduate: age 41: s. modern)

'We are very free of pressure—they leave us alone—we are really gorgeously free.' (Man graduate: age 62: grammar)

'I've done what I wanted to do—I've always had a completely free hand.' (Woman certificated: age 48: bilateral)

References to 'complete independence' and being left to do the job as they thought it should be done, were frequent. Of the eighty teachers interviewed, only three complained of having been seriously troubled by pressure. These three cases involved clashes in expectations concerning how a subject should be taught and occurred between young teachers and older members of the profession. One involved conflict with a head teacher—the other two with heads of department.

Teachers with high scores on this item tended to regard conflict of incompatible expectations as affecting particularly the young teacher, who was seen to be in an especially vulnerable position:

'This depends on the stage in one's career. The young teacher has a great problem here, bombarded in early days by all sorts of opinions.' (Man certificated: age 46: s. modern)

'For the young teacher, it can be hell.' (Man certificated: age 50: s. modern)

Despite these comments, a comparison of the scores of teachers in the twenty to twenty-nine age group with those of teachers in other age groups revealed no significant differences in role conflict experience.[1] This raises the interesting possibility that older teachers who claimed this as a serious problem for the young teacher were reflecting their own early experience of more restrictive and authoritarian conditions.

Out of 150 teachers, only twenty-eight scored high on personal experience of this conflict and of these, twenty-three taught in secondary modern schools. The basic reaction of these secondary modern teachers was one of irritation over the unwelcome flow of advice to teachers from various quarters and some took the view that head teachers and teachers were too amenable to the influence of these external agencies:

'Almost any magazine will tell parents how their children should be taught. The gutter press is keen on educating parents about their rights. Waves of fashionable thought are mediated through the HMIS.' (Woman graduate: age 30: s. modern)

'Everybody thinks they can teach. What annoys me is that some parents are full of advice—they think that they are the experts in teaching.' (Man certificated: age 41: s. modern)

'Too much in education is decided by outside influences. Many heads want a good ordered school for the governors and a free activity school for the inspectors. Head teachers are at fault here—they are swept along by external forces.' (Man certificated: age 50: s. modern)

Despite these comments, there were hardly any examples of the classic conflicts of American teachers. One of the few examples occurred in the very specialised context of religion teaching in a Catholic school:

'There is more conflict in teaching religion that in any other subject. There are the views of the parents, the priests and the college lecturers. You try to do many things which conflict. You try to please the parents—to give the idea of religion which they want—but this clashes with the new ideas in religion. In using new approaches you may come into conflict with the priests or with other teachers of religion.'

The role of the teacher of religion in Catholic schools in a time of rapid change in religious thinking seems likely to be exposed to the type of conflict mentioned here but it represents an exceptional case in the present inquiry.

Because conflicting expectations for the teacher's role exist in Britain without associated pressure, it was possible for some teachers to regard this situation as a stimulus rather than a problem. As one teacher put it: 'this is an aspect of the job which adds to its interest.'

It was clear therefore that exposure to incompatible expectations was not a serious problem or role conflict situation for the teachers. While incompatible expectations for the role were *seen* to exist, virtually no pressure to comply with these expectations was felt. The teachers gloried in their freedom of action and this sense of autonomy gave them considerable satisfaction.[2] Those who had high scores were in nearly every case expressing generalised irritation about the unwelcome number of opinions, rather than concern over pressure. There was no evidence that young teachers felt significantly more vulnerable than other teachers, although older teachers 'recollected' that it had been a problem. Some teachers, far from being irritated or troubled by a variety of expectations, saw this as a positive stimulus to discussion and to clarification of their own ideas about the teacher's role.

Professional status

Item (iv) had suggested conflict between the teacher's professional self concept and the way in which he was actually treated. Seventy-one of the 150 teachers in the sample saw this conflict as a problem of high importance, but schedule II revealed that of these only thirty-one had personally experienced such conflict to any degree. Twenty of these taught in secondary modern schools.

The great majority of teachers had not been personally troubled by feelings of conflict and vulnerability over their professional status. This 'non-vulnerable' group were composed of many heterogeneous elements and of many different orientations.

Professional confidence

Grammar-school teachers felt confident of their professional position and they had virtually no experience of having been regarded or treated in other than a professional way. Some of them, who felt that there was a problem in other sectors of the education system, suggested that lack of confidence among teachers was the basic reason for it:

'Professionalism is about confidence—it's up to the teachers.' (Man graduate: age 62: grammar)

'If you are unsure of yourself—you are likely to feel that you are not treated as other professional classes. If you are confident, you don't notice it. It may depend on a person's background and training.' (Man graduate: age 36: grammar)

The importance of professional confidence in this area was reiterated by teachers in other types of school. Some felt confident because their own professional preparation was longer than the usual period and for some, professional confidence was related to teaching a particular subject:

'Teachers do not behave as if they felt professional—they lack a really professional confidence in their own judgement—perhaps this is because of a lack of a sufficient level of education.' (Man certificated: age 56: s. modern)

'A longer Scottish professional training has given me a sense of confidence.' (Woman certificated: age 49: s. modern)

'The maths teacher is in a stronger position. In other subjects which are less precise—the teacher may be regarded with less status—but not in maths. Maths has helped my professional status. This position has been improved by modern maths—the parents find it a mystery!' (Man certificated: age 36: s. modern)

The non-aspirant

A frequent theme during the interviews was that there was too much concern about 'professionalism' in teaching, that individuals got the due they were worth and that the really important thing was the satisfaction to be obtained from the work. Such replies were however more characteristic of women than of men:

'People get what they ask for—some teachers are responsible for their own bad image. I've never expected much in the professional field—teachers expect too much.' (Woman certificated: age 48: bilateral)

'The important thing is self-satisfaction—whether I've done a good job in the class. I'm unconcerned about whether I'm regarded as equivalent to a shop keeper or a doctor by outsiders.' (Woman graduate: age 37: bilateral)

'I've no highfalutin' ideas of my own importance.' (Woman certificated: age 24: s. modern)

'I never look upon teaching as a profession—I'm just a worker. Many teachers feel they are on a higher level than anyone else—the idea of a profession is too high flown.' (Man certificated: age 56: s. modern)

It can be seen then that the factors of type of school, type and length of training, teaching subject and orientation to professionalism were important in explaining the responses of those teachers who felt little vulnerability on this issue.

Aspects of vulnerability

Among those who saw an important conflict related to professional status, or who had personally experienced such conflict, there was a tendency to answer in general rather than specific terms.

There were relatively few references to teachers having been treated unprofessionally by head teachers, inspectors or the local education authority. The remark by one teacher, that 'we are the last ones consulted in educational change—the system is run by laymen', did *not* represent a generally expressed sense of grievance. Similarly, although there were some pungent references to the role of the head teacher—'Heads too often treat staff as children'—these again were not representative of the majority.

It was clear from the interviews that the majority of teachers felt that they were both regarded and treated by their head teachers as professional persons, particularly in connection with their expertise in various subject fields. Problems and conflicts of professional status were attributed in the main to attitudes of the general public, particularly in the Midlands, and to a general decline in the status of the teacher as a result of social and economic change.

The local context and social change

Graham Turner in *The Car Makers* noted the effect which Midland affluence was having on some class attitudes—'We feel sorry for school teachers,' remarked a leading official of one of Coventry's largest trade unions. 'Our people have been earning their £30 a week for a long time.' As he pointed out, 'The old professional pillars of the community are regarded with pity, not awe.'[3] This attitude had been encountered and resented by some teachers, particularly those who had experience of other areas where they believed teachers were regarded with greater respect:

'A lot depends on the area. In the Midlands, teachers are regarded as of little significance—"the people who look after the kids"—whereas in Wales, teachers are looked up to as important in the community. The teacher there is a really telling force in the school and town. There is so much money here that education is not important.' (Woman graduate: age 30: s. modern)

In general, teachers in Wales, Scotland, Ireland, the home counties and the west country were seen as enjoying higher status and respect than the teacher in the English Midlands!

In addition to specifically local factors, the view was frequently expressed that the status of the teacher was declining as the result of increased numbers in the profession[4] and the growth in the size of communities. Teachers were seen to be 'so to speak, two a penny' and there were nostalgic references to the position of respect thought to have been enjoyed in the past by village and small town schoolmasters.[5]

Subject specialism

Mathematics teachers felt that their main subject specialism helped their professional status—others felt that their subject and their teaching role was undervalued and marginal. Teachers of woodwork, commercial and technical studies, domestic science, physical education and art mentioned problems and conflicts

67

arising from marginality. For some, these were role conflicts of immediate experience and as such they resulted in spirited comment. For others, the conflicts were in the main of past experience and they took the view that the situation was improving:

'A very sore point is the lack of professional regard from colleagues. The practical teachers are regarded as practical helpers, not teachers. We are used as a service department. The caretaking staff look on us as an adjunct to their function.'

'The attitude to craft teachers is changing for the better. There are better standards now—less drawing on industry and the use of more college trained men. Many staff remember being taught by the local carpenter—it will still take a generation to change attitudes completely.'

'Sometimes I'm made to feel that my particular subject is less "professional" than others. This was particularly true in the past —the attitude of *only* commercial subjects. The position is much better now—commerce is accepted—but the position can still be styled "instructor" rather than teacher.'

'I get the feeling that heads are not sympathetic to P.E.—a bit of a time filler—get rid of some surplus energy to concentrate on the real work. This is more so for girls than for boys. It is very irritating to have one's subject regarded in this way.'

In the sample as a whole, there were forty-two teachers of what may be called 'practical and creative arts'.* The fact that twenty-two scored high on perceived role conflict related to professional status, while twenty scored low, suggests a good deal of inter-school variation in this area. The attitude of colleagues was obviously important[6] as was also the attitude of the head teacher. Clearly some head teachers were careful to make all their staff feel that their role activities were significant, while in other schools, a particular academic or examination orientation caused certain teachers to feel that their activity was less significant. Reaction to this situation was expressed particularly forcefully by two art teachers:[7]

*Art, music, woodwork/metalwork, technical/commercial studies, domestic science/needlework, physical education.

'The teacher of the fine arts in this country is at a disadvantage. Culturally, we are a literary oriented society rather than a visual one.

The head should be aware of the role of art in the curriculum but nevertheless heads are wholly ignorant of the role of art. They have no understanding of its function educationally. Generally, we are always regarded as the odd men out—regarded as eccentric. No claims made by us are taken seriously.'

'Art in schools is treated as a "C" stream lesson—it is treated as a Cinderella. The head says "I'll give you the 'C' streams because they can do art."

I'm very keen on freedom in the art room but since the caretaker is the power this causes conflict. One spot of clay on the floor and there's trouble.'

Musgrove and Taylor (1969, p. 70) have suggested that subjects 'have become highly organized social systems with heavily defended boundaries'. They have suggested also that a secondary school teacher's self concept is very much bound up with his subject. Such an identification with the main teaching subject was generally apparent throughout this study and while in some cases this provided a sense of security for the teacher, in other cases it resulted in a sense of vulnerability and conflict.

Bureaucracy

A good deal of attention in sociology has focused upon the role conflicts of professionals in bureaucratic organisations. Within the school situation, the professional orientation of a teacher may conflict with bureaucratic requirements in two main areas—in the specialised activity of teaching within the classroom (or resource area) and in the formulation and execution of general school policy. It has already been shown that the teachers experienced hardly any conflict in the first area—their professional autonomy was virtually complete. Boyan (1969, p. 203) has argued that schools exhibit much more 'structural looseness' than is usual in bureaucratic organisations and this serves to preserve the teacher's autonomy. This was the case here.

Very little conflict was apparent also in matters relating to general school policy. A few teachers had strong feelings on this:

'In schools there is a hierarchy—decisions are made without consultation with all the professionals. The hierarchy in education as a whole ignores the teacher in the classroom', but for the majority there was no evidence of serious conflict between professional expectations and bureaucratic procedures. Most teachers seemed satisfied with the degree of professional consultation and shared decision-making in their schools. There was an impression (it can only be stated tentatively) that many staff were prepared to accept quite readily the head teacher's policy in general matters provided their autonomy in the classroom was untouched. Where a policy, such as non-streaming, had direct implications for the classroom, attitudes changed.

Some of the teachers showed explicitly an approach which Corwin (1965) has distinguished as characteristic of an 'employee' role rather than a professional role:

'I feel that I am employed by the head and I do feel that he has the ultimate say, although as a good employer he has a responsibility to ask the opinions of those who have to carry out the policy.

I am not angry about lack of participation because I have the feeling of an employee—I tend to accept things without too much fuss.'

'I've always tried, if it was possible, to carry out the wishes of authority—probably because I'm a member of the older generation.'

The absence of serious conflict over general school policies and bureaucratic procedures was clear. The reasons for this absence included the relatively small size of the schools, the amount of participation practised in some of them and the orientation of the teachers to questions of wider professional involvement.

Summary

In general, conflict arising from a sense of role vulnerability was to be found in its clearest form among secondary modern teachers. Basically, this conflict reflected marked differences in the teacher's evaluation of his role and profession and those of the general public with whom he interacted. Graduate teachers within such schools felt themselves to be less vulnerable in this respect and the indications are that the certificate in education as a professional qualification exposes its holders to a feeling of role vulnerability.

The importance of a secondary-school teacher's main specialism was also apparent as a factor in vulnerability and there was evidence that in some schools marginal status was still a reality for teachers of certain subjects.

There was virtually no evidence however that teachers in any type of school felt vulnerable or in conflict about pressure exerted upon them, lack of professional treatment or bureaucratic constraints. Above all, a sense of autonomy emerged as being the most prized possession of the British school teacher, the enjoyment of which prevented serious experience of role conflict in this area.

7 Commitment and conflict

Wilson (1962, p. 26) has argued that 'the strictly professional attitude—to remember that one's clients are just cases, so much stressed in medicine, law and social work—is simply not possible in teaching.' While this is an overstatement of the position, it is true to say that the importance of relationships and the idea of commitment to the welfare of pupils is much stressed in the professional preparation of teachers—especially in colleges of education. Graduate teachers are much less exposed (for reasons of shorter preparation among others) to this type of role socialisation, but even here, such teachers if they enter grammar schools are likely to meet with powerful expectations for 'loyalty to the school'—especially from older members of the profession. In other words, the majority of teachers find themselves faced with expectations for commitment—defined in some cases in terms of pupil welfare and in other cases in terms of organisational welfare. Basically, teachers are expected to stay 'for a reasonable period of time'* in order to develop the relationships thought necessary for the teaching process or to give some loyal service to the school as an organisation. These expectations for commitment clash however with a widespread belief in the profession that advancement and recognition goes to the man who moves frequently rather than to the man who gives evidence of commitment. In this way, a role conflict situation can be created for the teacher.

*Not less than two years for the young teacher, four to five years for others.

Similar conflicts have been shown to exist for other professional practitioners—for doctors (Ben-David 1958), nurses (Bennis, W. G. 1958) and university staff (Caplow and McGee 1958). Gouldner (1958) has investigated this type of role conflict for staff in a liberal arts college and Blau and Scott (1963) conflict for social workers, but there appears to have been no investigation of similar conflicts for school teachers.

The teachers in this inquiry saw conflict between commitment and career orientation as an important problem—64 per cent registering high scores on the perception schedule. 26 per cent of the sample registered high personal experience of such conflict but significant differences appeared when the scores for various categories of teacher were compared.

TABLE 5   *RCP and RCE: % of high scores in the commitment v. career orientation area[a]*

	RCP	RCE
(87) Men	64.3	37.9[e]
(63) Women	61.9	9.5
(83) Teachers[b]	60.2	25.3
(67) Teachers[c]	68.6	26.9
(69) S. modern	71.0	34.8[d]
(43) Grammar	53.5	13.9
(69) S. modern	71.0	34.8
(38) Bilateral	63.2	23.7
(39) Men s. modern	76.1	53.8[e]
(48) Other men	54.2	25.0
(30) Women s. modern	63.3	10.0
(33) Other women	63.6	9.1

[a]No significant differences were found between the scores of grammar- and bilateral-school teachers.
[b]Less than 10 years experience.
[c]More than 10 years experience.
[d]Significant differences in χ^2 test beyond the 5 % level.
[e]Significant differences in χ^2 test beyond the 1 % level.

Men and women

That men should have personally experienced significantly more role conflict than women teachers had been expected. Despite the campaigns of the Women's Liberation Movement, the cultural expectation that men will be 'achievers' is strongly entrenched. Less than 10 per cent of the women teachers had any considerable experience of this conflict. This suggests either lower levels of career aspiration among women teachers or a willingness and ability on their part to wait for promotion within one school, thus reducing the clash of commitment and career line. The majority of the women were married (65 per cent) and some referred explicitly to this fact as the reason for their low exposure to this type of conflict—'Being a married woman it is not so important to me to "get on"—I want to get to know a group of children—"getting on" is secondary.'

Of men teaching in secondary modern schools, 53.8 per cent registered a high level of personal experience of conflict between commitment and career orientation compared with only 25 per cent of men teaching in other types of secondary school (p <0.01). This highly significant difference within the male teaching group has important implications. It can be argued that the male secondary modern teacher, conscious both of the low status of the institution in which he works and of the low status and reward of his professional qualification (77 per cent were certificated), sees a greater need than other male secondary teachers for mobility to improve his career status. This need may also be reinforced by a more limited career structure within his existing school.[1] At the same time, the role socialisation of most secondary modern school teachers will have taken place within colleges of education where the emphasis will have been upon the affective aspects of teaching, particularly the importance of relationships. In this way, men certificated teachers in secondary modern schools are exposed to considerable role conflict. Their low status and salary necessitate career mobility (with associated movement among schools), while their socialisation for the teaching role has stressed stability and continuity of relationships with the pupils. Other men secondary teachers, predominantly graduate (83 per cent in this study) and teaching in schools possessing higher status and a greater range of career possibilities, are less acutely affected than their colleagues in secondary modern schools.

Complexity of variables

In analysing conflict between commitment (client and organisational) and career orientation in the teaching situation, a considerable number of variables have to be taken into account. An orientation towards commitment can result from a firmly held belief that the pupils need a sustained relationship with particular teachers and the belief also that schools operate more smoothly and efficiently where teacher turnover is small. On the other hand, such an orientation may represent a compensation by the teacher who has experienced lack of career success or who is unwilling, for a variety of reasons, to move from his existing situation.[2] A desire to stay and 'belong' may also represent a powerful psychological need of the person, contributing towards 'commitment' orientation. Similarly, a career orientation may result from the possession of marketable professional skills or qualifications, a belief that variety of experience is important as a developmental process, from sheer economic necessity or from a desire for power and influence. The desire to move—expressed as a fear of 'getting into a rut'—may also represent a psychological need contributing towards career orientation. It is obvious also that both these orientations can involve the operation of several of these factors simultaneously.

In addition to the complexities of individual motivation there are also structural factors to be considered. Important among these, as Blau and Scott (1963) have pointed out, are the amount of opportunity for advancement within a profession and the amount of opportunity within any given organisation. The teaching profession has experienced an increase in opportunities for advancement particularly as a result of the creation of head of department and special responsibility posts in schools since 1956. These opportunities however are available more liberally in large schools and in schools undertaking considerable advanced examination work.

High scorers

The interviews provided some kind of probe into the varieties of teacher reaction to conflicts of commitment and career. The 64 per cent who rated this conflict as of high importance divided roughly equally into two broad response patterns. The first group, composed mainly of men, exhibited strong feelings on this issue, generally as a result of their own personal experience of conflict. Essentially they took the view that relationships and continuity were very important in the teaching process and that the system of promoting and rewarding teachers favoured the wrong type of experience (variety of schools) rather than depth of experience in a particular school. Thus a man was faced with a severe conflict arising from his perception that continued service in one school was a handicap not a help to his career:

'Should one be loyal to one's students and give them continuity, or go glory- and cash-chasing around the country?' (Man certificated: age 53: s. modern)

'The people responsible for promoting teachers to headships equate "experience" with moving from school to school instead of moving from pupil to pupil; viz. person-centred teaching.' (Man graduate: age 34: bilateral)

'The "two-year gypsy" is probably the most unfortunate phenomenon of recent teaching history.' (Man certificated: age 50: s. modern)

'One has got to make a choice—one either stays without much hope of promotion—or one decides "I'm going up in the scale" and one moves. The problem is that people can't get promotion where they are.' (Man certificated: age 39: s. modern)

'If a person doesn't move in teaching he is regarded almost as a failure.' (Man certificated: age 29: s. modern)

'The position is terribly wrong that people feel they should have to move to get promotion. The teacher needs to be in a school at least three years before he is beginning to teach to the advantage of the pupils.

There is nothing more disastrous than the constant movement of teachers. Experience in this school is the same as experience in other schools—teaching children.' (Man certificated: age 36: s. modern)

'People of a slick, ruthless type achieve success, where more dedicated people who take a more moral view may not succeed.' (Man certificated: age 54: s. modern)

Associated with such reactions were various suggestions for a reform of the existing situation. Most commonly mentioned was a salary scale which rewarded the competent, dedicated teacher who had demonstrated his commitment to the pupils and to the school. Also mentioned was a system of promotion which did not take able teachers out of the classroom and into administration. As one teacher put it, 'You can always tell a successful teacher because he's not teaching.' A suitable career goal for those who wanted to remain actively teaching was suggested in the 'master teacher' role.[3] The existing system of head of department and special responsibility posts in schools was seen to be the cause of an undue amount of movement in the profession, making young men restless for their first S.R. post after one year's teaching.

The general impression of such interviews was that an entirely wrong system of values and priorities was operating in the career structure of teaching. The essential qualities of dedication, commitment and willingness to see through a project started, were being undervalued, while 'gadabouts', 'fly-by-nights' and 'two-year gypsies' achieved success.

The second group of high scorers, whilst seeing an important conflict between commitment and career, tended to react much less strongly to it. This was partly because they accepted it as an 'inevitable' problem reflecting more widespread changes in society. Some were prepared to accept that while commitment might be important to them, this position was not necessarily any more virtuous than other positions:

'It is a major problem—stability in schools is suffering badly— the curriculum—the pupils. But it's part of the increased general mobility in society—it's bound to happen. The trouble is that it hits more in teaching than in other things.' (Woman certificated: age 57: bilateral)

77

'The turnover of staff is considerable and while many new-comers do bring in fresh ideas and a breath of fresh air, the overall result is to prevent continuity and to stultify many progressive ideas.' (Man certificated: age 54: s. modern)

'Some of us feel committed—I always feel dreadfully committed to the people I teach. Others don't feel this—they are no less good as teachers because of this.' (Man certificated: age 46: s. modern)

'One stays put out of self-interest—one moves out of self-interest.' (Man certificated: age 46: s. modern)

Patterns of opportunity

Teachers in the older age range (over fifty) had been expected to see commitment-career conflict as important and generally to adopt a critical attitude to 'careerism'[4] in the profession. Of the twenty-five teachers in this age group, eighteen registered high scores on schedule I and some strong condemnation of careerism was forthcoming. On the other hand, some older teachers readily accepted that there was now much more opportunity for advancement than when they began their careers. The attitude of this group was *not* that the situation was professionally deplorable but that it was professionally different:

'At one time it was thought that remaining in one post was the thing to do, but now the more you hop about the more experience you gain. When I started this would have been frowned upon.' (Woman graduate: age 57: s. modern)

'In the thirties you hung on like grim death—now it's very easy to move.' (Man graduate: age 62: grammar)

Structural changes in the profession were recognised as important,[5] so also was the structure of opportunities within different schools. There was a greater consciousness among teachers in grammar and bilateral schools of the possibilities of internal promotion and there was evidence that able young men were retained in these schools by progressive salary increases in the form of graded posts. The irony of this situation was that while many teachers felt that continuity of staff was especially important for pupils in secondary modern schools, particularly the less able and those with disturbed home backgrounds, the structure of opportunities within these schools did not help such continuity.

Low scorers

The group of teachers who rated commitment-career conflict as of comparatively low importance included those who saw adequate career possibilities within their existing schools. Also among the low scorers were those who disclaimed ambition and career orientation, stressing the greater importance of stability for their families or their fortunate possession of other sources of income. The remainder, who clearly had some career orientation but were still low scorers in this conflict area, either attacked the generally accepted idea that promotion was closely associated with mobility among schools or, on the other hand, they stressed the positive advantages of teacher mobility:

'People who move seem to do well but people who stay also do well—it depends on the head's attitude—some reward variety of experience, some reward loyalty.

You have to achieve what you regard as relevant experience and find someone who agrees with you.' (Man certificated: age 28: bilateral)

'Mobility goes with the idea of professional practitioners. Mobility is an inevitable situation—experience is valuable and therefore the teacher ought to be mobile.' (Man graduate: age 25: s. modern)

'From middle age, teachers become the backbone of the school but before this gaining experience is important; it is a necessary part of learning.' (Man graduate: age 24: bilateral)

'There is a danger of becoming too committed to an institution —the school becomes your life.' (Man graduate: age 31: grammar)

A low score in this role conflict area could therefore indicate one of a number of reactions. It might indicate a lack of career orientation in which case no conflict with commitment would arise. On the other hand, a teacher with a career orientation would

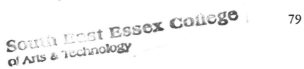

see little conflict if he was sceptical of the value of commitment and saw the advantages to the schools of teacher mobility. A low score could also indicate that a teacher saw ample career possibilities within his existing school or felt that neither commitment nor mobility provided any automatic advantage for career prospects.

Teacher mobility

A good deal of attention has been given in the sociology of organisations to the effects of succession and mobility and to the relationships between professionalisation and commitment (Grusky and Miller 1970). The result of studies has been to indicate the complexity of the field rather than to provide clear-cut answers. While some studies, particularly of small organisations, have suggested that 'succession is disruptive, typically producing low morale and conflict among the staff',[6] others have pointed to the functional effects for organisations of succession.

In education, statements of concern about the possible bad effects of high rates of teacher turnover are frequent (Central Advisory Council for Education (England), 1963 and 1967). There are relatively few references to the possibly functional effects of teacher turnover.[7] This reaction is the result of a widely held view that teachers cannot begin to give really effective service until they have been at a school for two years. Such a view stems directly from the importance attached, particularly in primary and secondary modern schools, to the establishment of affective relationships as the necessary context within which learning can take place.

If commitment and continuity are thought to be essential to the welfare of the pupils and the school, it seems reasonable to suppose that the salary and promotion structure of the teaching profession would reward such characteristics, given acceptable levels of individual professional competence. From the teacher's point of view they do not—reliance is placed instead upon the teacher having internalised 'commitment' during his professional preparation or having developed it as a personal moral value. The teacher, particularly in junior and secondary modern schools, is thus placed in a serious role conflict situation. Head teachers of course recognise this dilemma and many attempt to alleviate it by the judicious use of special responsibility payments[8] but small schools and those with little advanced work are at a disadvantage.

Professionalism and commitment

The work of Gouldner (1958) is frequently quoted in this connection, particularly regarding his distinction between 'cosmopolitans' and 'locals'. 'Cosmopolitans' are seen to be more committed to professional reference groups than to the employing organisation, while 'locals' are seen to be more committed to the employing organisation. It has been suggested that 'cosmopolitans' are more highly committed to professional skills than are 'locals'—hence the differences in their orientations. Blau and Scott (1963) have indicated the limitations of this model and the present inquiry provides further evidence of these limitations. In the teaching situation, while graduates tend to show a 'cosmopolitan' orientation and certificated teachers a 'local' orientation, these differences cannot be interpreted as showing differential commitment to professional skills. They reveal in fact different *concepts* of professional skill. The graduate emphasises the intellectual aspects of the teacher's role, the certificated teacher emphasises professional skills which are demonstrated in relationships.

Summary

Wilson's (1962) description of the clash between commitment and career orientation in teaching as 'a most significant role conflict' expressed the view of virtually two-thirds of the teachers. That it was seen as most significant was because the majority of teachers accepted the legitimacy of expectations for commitment while at the same time perceiving a close association between mobility and promotion. Thus the essential conditions for conflict were created.

In an attempt to resolve this dilemma many teachers suggested that a reasonable period of commitment could be defined as four to five years service in a school and that thereafter a teacher could with a clear conscience look for advancement in other schools. There was general condemnation of individuals who moved after only one or two years service (except in the case of young teachers just beginning their career). Such individuals were regarded as professionally irresponsible and disruptive to the schools and the fury of their critics was increased by the belief that such 'irresponsibles' were frequently promoted:

> All these ruddy people float into a school and float out again leaving all manner of hell after them. They often get on, because their sins don't catch up with them. It's hard to stay and sustain a piece of work—a teacher has to have the integrity to see the results of the work.

The brunt of the personal experience of this conflict fell upon men teaching in secondary modern schools. They, more than any other category of teacher, felt keenly the incompatibilities of the situation. Caught between their firm belief in the value of sustained relationships with the pupils and their pressing economic needs for promotion, they reacted with understandable bitterness. It was apparent that this discontent provided a powerful dynamic behind proposals for the reform of the salary and reward structure of the teaching profession.

8 Values and conflict

Teachers in the past have been more concerned with the inculcation of goodness than the development of cleverness. Their role has been characteristically that of custodian of traditional values and standards. Their primary function has been to ensure that certain moral, spiritual and cultural 'truths' were accepted and internalised by their pupils. To this end, the selection and professional preparation of teachers emphasised, as Taylor (1969a) has pointed out, the teacher's own identification with an appropriate set of values.

While a situation of general agreement existed in society as to what constituted right values and standards, the teacher's role as initiator of the young was relatively free from conflict. The teacher, with the minister and the priest, represented the superiority of revealed truth and like the religious was regarded as having a vocation to propagate this truth to the young. The gradual breakdown of value consensus in advanced industrial societies has however created a situation of considerable role conflict potential for the teacher. The values and standards which he has represented are increasingly questioned and even ridiculed. The mass media provide a powerful and attractive alternative source of guidelines for living. Parents continue to expect teachers to maintain traditional virtues (Musgrove and Taylor 1965) and yet the impression grows that the real business of society is conducted in very different terms.

Waller (1965, p. 34) has given a perceptive view of the parent-teacher relationship in this sphere:

Communities in general have chosen to use the schools as repositories for certain ideals…Among these ideals are those moral principles which the majority of adults more or less frankly disavow for themselves but want others to practise; they are ideals for the helpless, ideals for children and for teachers. There are other ideals which are nearly out of print because people do not believe in them any more. Though most adults have left such ideals behind they are not willing to discard them finally. The school must keep them alive. The school must serve as a museum of virtue.

For those teachers who personally endorse traditional values and standards and who accept that their function is basically a transmission of them to their pupils, any associated conflict is likely to be expected. Conflict with the prevailing tendencies of the culture will be a continuance of the 'missionary' and 'crusader' theme which has been a strong characteristic of the profession.[1] As such it can be expected to be a source of professional pride.

Concern however may be caused by the perception that the battle for traditional values is being lost, partly because of the powerful agencies working against the teacher's efforts and partly because of lack of effective support by parents for the teacher's position. Some teachers will be torn between their own conviction that they should maintain traditional values and their perception that such activity is apparently fruitless in terms of its effect upon the social system. Others may encounter very direct conflict with alternative value positions firmly held and vigorously argued by their own pupils. While it is true that many teachers have always encouraged their pupils to adopt a questioning attitude, it is also true that present day pupils do this with a confidence, skill and persistence (formerly called 'cheek') rarely seen in the past.

On the other hand, teachers who do not accept that their role implies a specific set of value commitments or who deal with value questions from a relative rather than an absolute standpoint, may find themselves in conflict with the expectations of parents, colleagues or head teachers.

King (1969) has drawn attention to the difficulties involved in defining values. In this study the phrase 'traditional values and

standards' (used in the role conflict schedules) was taken to mean
—honesty, truthfulness, consideration for others and the
acceptance of the basic tenets of Christian morality, as well as
concepts of good manners, respect for persons and property,
and endorsement of the work-success ethic. The conflict schedules
had suggested that teachers were expected to uphold such values
and standards as part of their teaching function (not necessarily
in their private lives) but at the same time it was suggested that
such values were increasingly ignored in society. Almost two-
thirds of the teachers saw value conflict defined in these terms,
as a problem of considerable importance, and 36 per cent indicated
that they had been personally troubled to a high degree by such
conflict. Analysis of the scores of different categories of teacher
revealed that older teachers and teachers in secondary modern

TABLE 6   *RCP and RCE: % of high scores in the value conflict
area[a]*

	RCP	RCE
(87) Men	60.9	35.6
(63) Women	66.7	34.9
(83) Teachers[b]	57.8	28.9
(67) Teachers[c]	70.1	44.7[d]
(69) S. modern	68.1	47.8[d]
(43) Grammar	65.1	25.6
(69) S. modern	68.1	47.8[d]
(38) Bilateral	52.6	26.3
(39) Men s. modern	74.3	56.4[e]
(48) Other men	50.0	18.8
(30) Women s. modern	60.0	36.7
(33) Other women	72.7	36.4

[a]No significant differences were found between the scores of grammar and bilateral
school teachers.
[b]Less than 10 years experience.
[c]More than 10 years experience.
[d]Significant differences in χ^2 test beyond the 5 % level.
[e]Significant differences in χ^2 test beyond the 1 % level.

schools had most experience of this type of conflict. Older teachers could be expected to identify more closely than younger teachers with traditional values and standards and their greater exposure to this type of role conflict is hardly surprising. The findings support Spindler's (1963) suggestion of the greater vulnerability of older teachers in a situation of value change.

Similarly it is clear that secondary modern school teachers are faced with a greater value gap between themselves and their pupils than is the case in other types of secondary school and their higher conflict scores indicate the consequences of this situation.

Men teachers in secondary modern schools

The significantly higher RCE scores for men teaching in secondary modern schools when compared with men teaching in other secondary schools are particularly noteworthy—especially when no such differences are to be found between women teaching in secondary modern schools and women teaching in other types of school. They suggest (and the interviews bear this out) that men teaching in secondary modern schools see their role very much in terms of upholding traditional values and standards while at the same time they find a considerable challenge to these values and standards from the boys for whom they take a major responsibility in the schools. In contrast to this, men teaching in other types of school showed less consistent identification with traditional values and standards and had less direct experience of serious value differences with their pupils. The work of Musgrove and Taylor (1969) has shown important differences in the role concepts of different categories of men teacher and these differences are clearly related to this type of role conflict exposure.[2]

Value components

A main focus of interest in this area of conflict might be said to lie not so much in the broad differences between various categories of teacher, as in the examination of teacher reaction to specific value components included in 'traditional values and standards'. The interviews revealed that high scorers were particularly concerned with perceived trends in society working against honesty and truthfulness, respect for persons and property and appropriate attitudes to work.

Honesty

A frequently reiterated theme among teachers in all types of school was the decline in standards of honesty:

'In modern society one is aware that the school is an island—it sets values which are foreign to their experience.

There's a dreadful problem of standards of honesty—a great deterioration over the last twenty years. The teacher has an increasingly difficult role to perform in view of the general slackness in society.' (Man certificated: age 59: s. modern)

Many teachers took the view that pupils were only too well aware that 'knocking things off' was a widespread and accepted feature of life outside the school and the teacher's attempt to assert another value position was seen as evidence of naivety.

Respect

Wider social developments were also seen to be working against the teacher's efforts to establish the value of 'respect'.[3] Many teachers were clearly concerned with this problem on two levels —a general one, involving ideas of respect and consideration for people in general, and a specific one involving respect for teachers in particular! 'There is a problem of respect—for what the teacher stands for rather than for the person. There is much less respect for the office of teacher. We stood in awe of our teachers—this was not necessarily good but things now have gone too far.' Older teachers in particular tended to see a decline in such indicators of respect as good manners and courtesy and a decline in respect for institutional (rather than personal) authority. Insofar as teachers attempted to uphold traditional standards of courtesy or ideas of respect for certain status positions they saw themselves to be in conflict with the climate of the times. There was however no sense of crisis in the teachers' own authority position (or none was admitted), but changing concepts of respect were seen as making the teachers' role more difficult to perform in modern society.[4]

Thrift, property and the work ethic

The traditional Puritan values of thrift and careful use of property have been a strong feature of state education in Britain. This has arisen partly as a result of the value orientations of the social groups from which many teachers originated and partly from sheer economic necessity. Many senior persons in education have been socialised in a Gladstonian ethos of retrenchment and economy,[5] and have internalised the related values. It is no surprise to find therefore that many teachers were concerned about the cavalier attitude to property which the affluent society was apparently encouraging among the young. There were frequent complaints that pupils placed no value on property, public or private, and teachers were appalled at the casual attitude of pupils towards expensive items such as watches and record players.

A related question involved concern over lax attitudes to work on the part of the pupils. In particular, many secondary modern school teachers were disturbed by what they regarded as the growth of easy-going attitudes to life among their pupils and a questioning of the value of work:

'Many pupils are coming to hedonistic conclusions about life. The thing that disturbs me most is their attitude to work—"I'm not going to work"—the view of work as a hateful thing—an avoidance of the difficult and boring.

They take this view because there are no sanctions for the non-worker—the net of the Welfare State holds everybody up.' (Man certificated: age 54: s. modern)

'There is the issue of work—we say a job ought to be done well—this is a standard teacher's saying. They find that a great many adults don't work very hard and don't maintain high standards in what they do.' (Man certificated: age 56: s. modern)

'There is a "couldn't care less attitude"—"I shall get by"—the importance of work is secondary—and without work they do get by! Some people argue that work itself has no value—what an attitude!' (Man certificated: age 62: s. modern)

Hargreaves (1967) and others have drawn attention to the conflict in values which occurs between teachers and pupils in secondary modern schools. The 'work ethic' is an important factor in this conflict. Historically, teachers in the elementary and secondary modern school tradition have attempted to carry the gospel of work-related virtues to a population whose perceptions of work and society have made it sceptical about such virtues. Such conflict then is a long-standing tradition. What has changed is the social context of the conflict. Teachers in the past whose school-rooms bore the legend 'He who will not work, shall not eat' knew this to be a reality, and both pupils and teachers were very conscious of the ideology of work. The Welfare State and the growth of the ideology of non-work has radically changed the situation, allowing pupils to dispute the teacher's values and creating a feeling among some teachers that society's values are moving more in the direction of the pupils' than of the teacher's.[6]

Sexual morality

There was surprisingly little reference to questions of sexual morality.[7] The few teachers who expressed concern about changing standards felt that the instant gratification syndrome which they perceived in modern society was having undesirable effects on the sexual behaviour of young people: 'There is too much instant gratification—they want the tape recorder and the motor bike now—this carries over into sex behaviour—they must be gratified now. Society is responsible for this.'

The school and values

There is no doubt that the majority of teachers saw their role in a value conflict situation with powerful tendencies in the culture. For many, this was a personal struggle since their own endorsement of traditional values was involved. It was also a professional struggle, since they saw maintenance of such values and standards as part of the teacher's duty and believed that parents expected them to take a stand on such matters. The essence of this view was expressed in a belief that with the decline in the influence of the church, the position of the school on value questions was now crucial: 'Part of the teacher's job is to maintain high standards in the face of a slackening in society as a whole. If they don't get the standards from the school, where will they get them?' There was some feeling of bitterness, however, that teachers were being 'used' by parents to uphold values and standards which the parents themselves lacked the moral courage to uphold directly. There was also some feeling of betrayal in that parents failed to back up the action taken by teachers in defence of traditional values.

The major issues in value conflict were honesty, truthfulness, respect for persons and property and appropriate work attitudes. An important secondary theme which emerged during the interviews, focused upon appropriate standards of dress and concepts of loyalty to the school.

Appearance and loyalty

Favouring short hair rather than long, trousers rather than jeans and school uniforms rather than other forms of dress, may be said to be value judgments. Many teachers held these value judgments, felt that standards of appearance were important and were conscious of a growing pressure against these standards. Basically, their position was that the traditional standards of appearance expected in schools were 'appropriate' and 'business-like' and prepared the pupils realistically for the expectations of future employers. There was also a tendency, on the part of some, to see dress as indicative of a wider set of values.

At the same time, some teachers realised that questions of dress and appearance could become major sources of alienation between themselves and the pupils, and as a consequence they were prepared to re-examine their views. Others however believed in taking a firm stand and were hostile to those younger teachers whose own appearance was taken to identify them with the pupils rather than with the staff.

Loyalty to the school was another value position where many teachers found themselves in conflict with a changing social ethos. Grammar-school teachers in particular stressed this aspect of value conflict, although it was mentioned by teachers in all types of school. Such teachers found a decline in loyalty to the school and a weakening of the idea that it was an honour to represent the school.[8] The issue tended to crystallise upon playing for the school team and for this reason teachers of physical education and those teachers concerned with games had most experience of it:

'There should be more idea of loyalty to an institution. There is a pull for boys between the school and their own interests. Some boys are selected for a team but would rather play for another team, help on a market stall or play soccer rather than rugger.' (Man graduate: age 40: grammar)

'There is less loyalty to the school now—when I first came it was a thrill to turn out for the school.' (Woman certificated: age 37: grammar)

'They put going into town before playing for the school—whereas when I was at school nothing would stand in the way of playing for the school.' (Woman certificated: age 26: s. modern)

For those teachers who had internalised loyalty to the school as an important value, growing evidence of a casual attitude to it on the part of the pupils was disturbing and irritating.

Social concern

Although the majority of teachers saw important value conflicts in their work, they did not see an entirely black picture. While recognising that many of the values which teachers sought to uphold were under attack, often by their own pupils, they recognised also certain positive aspects of the situation. Teachers saw a decline in aspects of formal respect for persons but many pointed to a developing sense of social concern among their pupils for the poor, the handicapped and the old. They commended also the fact that present-day adolescents were thinking for themselves and questioning value positions much more than pupils had done in the past. This questioning attitude, seen by teachers as an intellectual virtue, unfortunately however seemed to lead to value conclusions of which they did not approve!

Younger teachers

Of the 150 teachers, fifty-five registered low conflict scores in the value area on schedule I. Of these, forty-five were teachers under the age of forty. Teachers with low conflict perception scores tended to question or reject the premise that they were expected to uphold traditional values and standards as part of their role obligation. They were often critical of the values and standards regarded as important in schools and stressed the necessity for complete honesty and frankness when value questions were discussed:

'Are we expected to maintain traditional values and standards? Surely not. If we are expected to do so, we ought not to be.' (Woman graduate: age 29: s. modern)

'I have not been appointed to teach a set of standards—they will not have been specified in my appointment.' (Man graduate: age 34: bilateral)

'It doesn't matter what your views are as long as you are honest—this is better than one patterned front from the teachers.' (Man graduate: age 36: bilateral)

'The traditional value of "getting on" expressed in schools—I think it's materialistic—it really means making a lot of money.' (Man certificated: age 28: s. modern)

'Take assembly for instance. As a person concerned with Christianity I find it very damaging and morally indefensible—tacit compulsion is involved. Compulsory worship is grotesque in the extreme.'

'Certain expected traditional values are nothing more than the fads and fashions of the period when many teachers and parents were young.' (Man graduate: age 36: grammar)

Since such teachers recognised no expectation that they should uphold a particular set of values and standards against attack, they registered little of the conflict which their colleagues perceived and felt. They were prepared to take a much more open (or less committed) position and to be flexible on value questions. Some however recognised that there were limits to this flexibility. As one young teacher put it: 'I don't feel a positive expectation to uphold traditional standards but I know there would be trouble if I maintained a totally opposite view.'

While the majority of low scorers attacked the suggestion that they were expected to uphold traditional values, a few attacked the problem from the other end. These teachers denied the reality of the teacher in value conflict with a permissive society by rejecting the suggestion that society was permissive. For these teachers, young people were different, not worse, and society was franker, not more lax.

Value conflict and adaptation

Spindler (1963) has suggested that teachers in the value conflict situations of modern industrial societies will make one of four possible reactions. Some will retreat into ambivalence and uncertainty and avoid situations where value questions are discussed. Others will react by identification with 'progressive' values and 'group thinkism' as a means of establishing good relationships with their pupils. An opposing 'compensatory' reaction will involve some teachers in taking a hard line traditionalist position and a posture of defending the ancient virtues. The 'adapted' teacher will come to terms with the conflict situation and attempt some kind of workable synthesis of traditional and emergent values.

There were examples of all four patterns during the interviews and inevitably reactions which did not correspond with any of these 'ideal types'. The general impression was that the majority of teachers were attempting some synthesis of different value positions[9] but there was evidence also that some senior teachers in influential positions in the schools favoured a firm reassertion of all traditional values and standards and regarded with hostility younger teachers who sought any modification of them.

Summary

Teacher role conflict in the value area was essentially a conflict with 'society' rather than with self. The majority of teachers saw themselves engaged in a value struggle with powerful external agencies—a struggle which they felt they were progressively losing, mainly because parents did not support them effectively. While teachers in all types of school saw such conflict, teachers in secondary modern schools, particularly men, felt most keenly the direct impact of this conflict. A minority of teachers, mainly young, saw and felt no such conflict with society. For them, conflict on value questions was more likely to occur within the school, between their orientations and those of senior teachers and head teachers. It may be that this type of conflict will become more significant in the future.

9 The head teachers

If the school as an organisation is viewed as a system of inter-locking roles, it is clear that any attempt to study teacher role conflict must take into account the role concepts and role behaviour of head teachers. These represent very important dimensions in the situation. As Hoyle (1969, p. 47) points out, 'there is no doubt that the climate of the British school is to a large extent shaped by the manner in which the head teacher perceives and performs his role.'

A good deal of attention has been given to leadership behaviour in various organisational settings, as it relates to such factors as job satisfaction of individuals in the organisation and to effects upon group morale (Katz and Kahn 1966). Recently, such approaches have been increasingly applied in educational settings, particularly in America (Gross and Herriott 1965; Halpin 1966). These studies show the considerable implications which leadership behaviour can have for teacher morale and professional performance. At the same time, problems of methodology have been revealed. For instance, how a head teacher or principal says that he conceives of his role may bear very little relation to how he actually behaves. On the other hand, the use of subordinates as 'observers' of leadership behaviour can be very unreliable.[1] In attempting to determine the 'true' behaviour of head teachers both measures are however clearly desirable.

In this study, the teachers' perceptions of the heads' behaviour in relation to the potential conflict areas had been obtained during the interviews. Subsequently, one hour focused interviews with the head teachers of the ten schools involved were used to obtain direct information on the heads' role concepts and role behaviour. Teacher perceptions and head teacher responses are presented for each of the four role conflict areas under investigation.

Role diffuseness and 'recognition'

Since important aspects of a teacher's achievement may be visible only to colleagues within the same school, the teachers were asked whether they felt that sufficient recognition of staff effort and achievement was given by the head teacher. The majority were in fact satisfied with the amount of recognition received from head teachers either in the form of public or private praise or in more tangible forms such as salary additions. Those who were dissatisfied, generally complained that the head teacher was too preoccupied with administrative work so that recognition of staff effort was neglected.

Head teachers were asked (a) if they saw it as part of their role to provide some form of verbal recognition of staff effort or whether they regarded this as primarily the business of the head of department—or (b) whether they took the view that 'mature professional persons don't need this sort of recognition'. Six of the head teachers claimed that recognition of staff effort was an important part of their role, two were undecided and two felt strongly that mature professional persons did not need or expect such recognition.

The 'praisers' felt that it was important for a teacher to know that his efforts had been noticed by the head teacher and that this might help to resolve any feelings of uncertainty or ambiguity concerning achievement. The general view taken by this group was that 'everyone is better for praise',[2] and they were often concerned that administrative duties prevented them from giving as much attention to this aspect of their role as they would wish.

Of the two head teachers who were undecided on this issue, one felt that teachers wanted to see the head teacher take an interest in their work rather than give praise as such, while the other had 'never really sorted this out' but felt that he did not reward verbally as much as he should (there was evidence however in this case that the head teacher's use of graded posts as a reward for staff effort was taken by his staff as an acceptable sign of 'recognition'). The two head teachers who took the view that verbal recognition by them was unnecessary felt that professionals did not need this type of incentive and might indeed resent it. There was no evidence that teachers in these two schools were more dissatisfied over recognition than their colleagues in other schools.[3]

The majority of the head teachers felt that heads of department should also provide recognition of staff effort within their departments and that this was particularly appropriate in the case of young teachers who might be in especial need of encouragement. There was no sense however of the head teachers delegating their 'recognition functions' to heads of department—they saw such action as essentially supplementary to their own. This situation may be taken to reflect the relatively small size of the schools as organisations, where the head teacher was in a position to know the details of staff activity and where departmental structures were not highly developed.

The role concepts held by the majority of the head teachers stressed the importance of recognition of staff effort. In so far as they put these concepts into practice, it is clear that they were able to reduce feelings of role ambiguity and role conflict among their staffs. The growing burden of administration and the increasing size of schools were however seen as threatening this situation in the future.

Role vulnerability

The role behaviour of head teachers has obvious implications for any feelings of vulnerability among their assistant staff over professional status. If the head teacher perpetuates in any sense the historic tradition of *the* qualified professional dealing with semi-professionals, then teacher role conflict can be expected to be high.

The teachers were asked whether they felt they had been treated as 'professional practitioners' by their head teachers. As reported in chapter 6, the majority perceived the head teacher as relating to them in a professional manner, particularly in the amount of autonomy which they enjoyed. Those who were dissatisfied were mainly, but not entirely, teachers who felt that their particular subject specialism was not given professional parity with other subjects in the school.

Head teachers were asked whether they saw it as part of their role to encourage the selection of certain teaching material or the adoption of certain teaching methods—or whether they felt that this was essentially the responsibility of the individual teacher. They were also asked what action they would take if they felt dissatisfied with the performance of a particular teacher.

With regard to teaching material and teaching methods, two head teachers saw their role as *'primus inter pares'*, giving virtually complete autonomy to their staff, four adopted a modified version of this role, while the remaining four took a more positive, interventionist approach. Those holding the *'primus inter pares'* role felt that highly qualified professionals knew what they were about and that 'the head's role here is self-effacement'. The four head teachers holding a modified version of this role agreed that professionals must be given considerable autonomy but felt that the head had some positive responsibilities in this area. These responsibilities were seen to include holding a watching brief, particularly on the work of younger teachers and encouraging the introduction of new methods in the school by suggesting possibilities or posing questions.[4]

The four 'positive interventionists' saw the head teacher's role in more defined terms. Two stressed that if examination results were unsatisfactory, direct action would have to be taken by the head teacher to change the syllabus, the approach to it or, if necessary, the staff responsible for it. One held firmly to a traditional view of the head teacher as having competence in a number of fields and of being able to operate and intervene in various subject areas as necessary.[5] One felt that the head teacher had a responsibility to be an educationist rather than an administrator and to give positive staff leadership in this area, subject to a proper regard for individual professional competence.[6]

Where a teacher's professional performance was seen to be unsatisfactory, the majority of head teachers indicated a cautious approach to the problem. Two admitted that they tended to take no action other than making their disapproval apparent and hoping that the teacher in question would move. They felt reluctant to face the unpleasantness of the situation and were concerned about the possible hurt to the feelings of the teacher, particularly if the teacher was no longer young. Two suggested that they approached such problems indirectly by suggesting that the teacher might like to see interesting work that was being done in another school or by suggesting that perhaps the teacher found certain restrictions in the school, e.g. lack of resources. The remainder indicated that they would act through the appropriate head of department and that such responsibility for teacher performance was primarily the latter's—'what they are paid their allowances for'.

In general, therefore, the role behaviour of the majority of the head teachers created the conditions in which teachers felt that they were treated as professionals and this feeling clearly contributed towards the low role conflict scores in this area. If anything, it could be said that the head teachers erred on the side of autonomy and freedom for their teachers, so that even cases giving serious cause for professional concern were treated in a non-directive way.[7]

Commitment and career

64 per cent of the sample of teachers had rated this conflict as of high importance in the teaching situation and 26 per cent had been personally troubled to a considerable degree by such conflict. Those teachers who had strong feelings about this conflict, and who felt that a wrong system of values dominated the reward structure in teaching, tended to be critical of 'the system' rather than of head teachers as such. 'The system', which was at fault, was seen to include the salary structure in teaching (including special responsibility allowances), the existence of appointing committees composed of laymen and, to some extent, the influence of the local education office. These aspects of the system were seen to work in favour of the 'mover' rather than the committed teacher.

Many teachers expected the head teacher to 'fight the system' and to work to ensure justice for the committed teacher. There was a general feeling that head teachers did what they could to ensure reasonable rewards for their loyal teachers but external forces were seen as being often more powerful than the head teacher. The position was complicated however by the fact that young men in particular felt that the head teacher should reward merit rather than loyal service, and where a head teacher was seen to reward loyalty there was some dissatisfaction among the younger staff who claimed that merit was more important than loyalty.

Head teachers were asked what relative emphasis they gave to 'commitment' on the one hand and 'variety of experience' on the other, when they were making an appointment or allocating an allowance. They were also asked what general importance they attached to the idea of commitment by staff to a school.

Seven of the head teachers claimed that, given reasonable competence in the individual, they favoured the committed teacher and would make internal promotions if this was possible. Three indicated that they kept their options open in this matter.

The seven 'commitment-rewarding' heads stressed the value of continuity in the life of schools and deplored the increase in teacher mobility. Mobility was seen to have bad effects upon pupil behaviour, academic achievement and staff morale. These head teachers expected two or three years service from a young teacher and about five years service from a head of department. Four of these head teachers claimed that their policy of rewarding commitment and loyalty was known to their staffs.

The three 'open option' head teachers, while recognising the value of continuity in schools, stressed also the functional nature of movement by teachers. The need for teachers to develop professionally through new experiences and challenges was mentioned and also the fact that able young teachers should be positively encouraged to move in their own career interests. One head teacher stressed that 'commitment every day' was the important thing, not necessarily years of service and that those teachers who stayed only a short time might still contribute a good deal to a school.

In general, however, the majority of the head teachers emphasised the value of commitment, loyalty and service from their staff over a number of years and claimed where possible to reward it. The teachers, in the main, perceived this to be so and felt that role conflict in this area was the result of structural and extra-school factors rather than of the head teacher's policies.

Values

A similar situation existed in relation to value conflicts. The majority of the teachers saw their role to be in value conflict with 'society', the influence of mass media and the growing permissiveness of many parents. There was little evidence of teacher–head teacher conflict over value questions. In the few cases where it did exist, it tended to involve young teachers and centred upon different evaluations of such factors as the importance of examinations, ideas of appropriate dress and appearance and the value of school assembly.

The head teachers were asked if they saw their role and that of their assistants as involving the maintenance of traditional values and standards in the face of growing scepticism. They were asked also if they felt they would have to take any action if a member of their staff held non-traditional or radical views in the fields of religion, politics or sexual morality, and if these views were known to the pupils.[8]

In response to the first question, all the head teachers felt that the school had a positive duty to transmit traditional values and standards to the pupils. This was however expressed in a number of ways and with different emphases:

'We try to set up the cardinal virtues—personal responsibility within the community—care of their own and other people's property. Parents expect you to maintain standards.'

'As far as I'm concerned—the old-fashioned line. The teacher ought to know what is right and wrong—or not be a teacher. There are too many people in education dithering about this.'

'One has to be firm about certain Christian standards—particularly those essential to human happiness.'

'If we don't give them the right sense of values—no-one else will. We have the job that the parents won't do and the church can't do.'

'I favour a firm stand—the nearer you move to them—the nearer you are to the next step. I'm concerned about the situation in higher education. If you stand to an absolute rather than a relative, you get nearer to something to which people can cling.'

While asserting their traditional responsibilities with varying degrees of firmness, almost all of the head teachers accepted the need for frank and honest discussion of value differences with senior pupils and there was evidence that speakers were invited to present different value perspectives in most of the schools. Some felt however that the situation was different with the less able pupils. As one put it, 'you should not put value alternatives to children not of the mental calibre to deal with them.'

Whether a head teacher should take any action when a teacher's non-traditional or radical views on religion, politics or sex were known to the pupils, touched a very sensitive area in school life, involving a number of important issues. Most of the head teachers claimed to have had little direct experience of such a situation occurring but they accepted that it posed a serious potential conflict situation. The essence of the conflict was that the head teachers felt that assistants must answer all questions honestly— but that in this case they would be troubled by what the teacher was 'honestly' saying.

Their concern arose for a number of reasons. They would be personally troubled because such views ran counter to views which they held as being central to the educative process. They would be professionally troubled because they feared indoctrination of such views, especially if political, and they were worried about possible dangerous repercussions on their pupils of a teacher's radical views on, for instance, sex or drugs. They felt that 'controversial' value positions would be contrary to the expectations of the majority of parents to whom they had a responsibility.[9]

It was apparent that some head teachers were able to avoid such a situation arising by careful selection of staff at interview. Individuals holding views thought to be seriously 'disruptive' to the ethos and values of the school would not be appointed and four of the head teachers attributed their lack of experience of this conflict largely to their interview policies.[10] In the event of such a situation arising, all the head teachers felt that they might have to intervene, depending upon the nature of the radical views expressed by a teacher. As one put it: 'In this situation, the role of the head is very difficult—caught between a belief in the pursuit of the truth and the expectations of the parents.'

Head teachers were not a considerable source of value conflict for their assistants, except in the case of some young teachers. Such intra-school conflict on value questions seemed to be avoided by the operation of a number of factors.[11] Important among these were the creation and maintenance of a good deal of consensus on values by the appointment policies of head teachers and the fact that any value differences which did exist could find their expression in the virtually private and autonomous world of the classroom. The fact that British schools, unlike American, have no tradition of close parental involvement in school affairs seemed to be a factor of importance in accounting for the low incidence of serious value conflict. Head teachers felt free to use their discretion in dealing with such problem situations without the pressure of organised parental opinion.

With regard to the emphasis given to different aspects of the teacher's role, the head teacher may be, as Musgrove and Taylor (1969, p. 55) conclude, 'a major source of conflict for teachers'. With regard to the four role conflicts investigated here, they were not a major source of conflict. That this was so, may be attributed partly to the way in which head teachers conceived of and performed their role in relation to their staff, partly to a tendency among teachers to see their problems resulting from extra-school factors such as 'the system' and 'society' and partly to the characteristics of British schools as organisations, where conflict can be contained in the 'buffer zone' of professional autonomy.

10 Conclusions and implications

The sociologist, some would argue, should present his results and conclusions and leave the implications to others. As Rex (1961, p. viii) points out, 'The sociologist qua sociologist, is in no better position than the layman to say whether or not a particular social end is to be desired.' However, to stop short at implications is to accept the 'Ivory Tower' role and to ignore completely the expectations which practical men have for the sociological enterprise. Bernstein (1961, p. 288) has remarked that 'whilst the sociology of education is concerned with rather more than the vicissitudes of the teaching situation…Those engaged in the practical business of education want an answer relevant to their day to day problems.' In so far as the following pages deal with implications rather than conclusions they do not represent sociological 'answers' to the problems of the teaching situation. They represent possible courses of action that seem desirable to one individual. Others may see different implications and alternative courses of action.

A question of 'results'

The majority of secondary school teachers in this study did not find role diffuseness—operationalised in terms of knowledge of results—to be a major source of strain or conflict. This was so because they saw 'results' and satisfying feedback from their efforts in role performance. Evidence of pupil response to their teaching, examination results, work with the sixth form and visits and letters from former pupils were the principal constituents of their sense of achievement and their principal defence against feelings of uncertainty. Those teachers who were deprived of any of these indicators, or whose experience of them was slight, tended to register high conflict scores. In practice, this meant that the majority of high scorers were teachers in secondary modern schools.

This latter finding, taken together with the evidence of Hargreaves (1967) and Bacchus (1967), suggests that teachers who are working with average and below average pupils for most of the time need to have some external source of reassurance and recognition[1] of their efforts. This is not to say that there is no satisfying response from their pupils—it is to recognise that such response is often obtained only after considerable input of nervous and physical energy on the teacher's part and that even after such effort non-response may be encountered more frequently by these teachers than by their colleagues.[2] The secondary-school teacher who does not teach the sixth form, whose pupils are not entered for external examinations and have no tradition of coming back to school after leaving age, has to rely very much upon his own sense of achievement based upon his own measures and impressions.[3] For some this is sufficient, for others there is a sense of uncertainty and conflict. What has been accomplished? The response to this situation may take the form of a steady growth in pessimism and cynicism over the years[4] and the creation of a progressively less stimulating learning environment. This suggests the desirability of ensuring that teachers in such situations and with such needs do receive recognition.

'Recognition functions' in the school

As has been shown, some head teachers are aware of staff needs in this area and stress the importance of the 'recognition function' in their role. They are aware too of the important role which the various heads of department could play in providing feedback to teachers. Such activity, effective within the limits of this study, had nevertheless an *ad hoc* quality rather than the characteristics of formulated policy. With far-reaching changes taking place in the schools, particularly affecting size and complexity of organisation, it can be suggested that the time has come for a more formulated approach to 'recognition function'. The roles of inspector and advisor for instance could incorporate functions of recognition and feedback more explicitly than they do at present and might operate, where appropriate, at head of department and even head teacher level. Within the school, these functions could also be made more explicit in the role of the head teacher and the head of department.

The work of Gross and Herriott (1965) has shown that a principal's conscious attempt to improve the performance of his teachers—his 'executive professional leadership'—can be very successful in achieving this goal, as well as having beneficial effects on teacher morale and pupil performance. If a head teacher explicitly includes in his concept of 'executive professional leadership' the need to provide feedback and recognition to staff with particularly difficult teaching assignments, then similar beneficial effects for the teacher, the pupil and the school may well result.

Such a function does assume however that the head teacher can obtain reliable information about a teacher's work without infringing the highly prized autonomy of the teacher. It assumes moreover that verbal recognition from the head teacher will be significant to the teacher.[5] Where academic and technical matters are involved, verbal recognition from the head teacher may be seen by specialists to be pleasant but not significant, because the head teacher is regarded as an amateur in the field. Clearly, however, the head teacher of a small school will have many opportunities to assess a teacher's work and contribution, albeit in indirect ways and in general terms.[6] The conditions of the large secondary school suggest that 'recognition functions' should be the concern of both the head teacher and the head of department. The latter may in some cases be in a better position to evaluate the teacher and his technical opinion may be more highly regarded by some staff.

Consequences of educational and organisational change

The realisation that teachers obtain satisfaction from their perception of particular 'results' suggests that the effect of educational and organisational change upon these perceptions needs to be closely studied. In other words, there is a need for 'planned change' in educational organisations[7] which monitors the consequences of innovation not solely in measures of learning achievement or pupil reaction but also in terms of teacher reaction and teacher satisfaction. While it is clear that educational systems do not exist merely to provide teachers with maximum satisfaction—it is equally clear that attempts at innovation which assume that the teacher will 'fit in' with the latest blueprint are doomed to failure. Any serious attempt to introduce change needs to be accompanied by an assessment of probable consequences for the teacher, programmes of reorientation and preparation and on-going monitoring of actual consequences. This may appear to be self-evident but it can be argued that modern educational systems in bringing the pupil rightly to the centre of the stage may have pushed the teacher too far into the wings—so that an explicit statement of the need to study the consequences of change for teachers is necessary.

Specifically, current attempts to make the teacher's role more diffuse through the inclusion of social work functions must take into account the possibility of increased role strain and role conflict for the teacher.

The reaction of teachers involved in new and generally more diffuse approaches to teaching and learning is also worthy of close study. It is known that changes in job design have implications for employee motivation[8] and some study of the implications of changes in the teacher's 'job design' seems desirable. This investigation has suggested that teachers in new and open learning situations generally perceive a higher level of interest among their pupils (which is very satisfying) but they are also in some uncertainty about actual learning achievements. Unless fairly specific efforts are made to assess and evaluate the results of these new approaches it may be that once the high initial enthusiasm has abated, teacher motivation may decline, resulting in a return to traditional patterns.[9]

Changed organisational contexts and their effect upon the teacher's perception of results, is another important area for research. Former grammar-school teachers operating in the context of a comprehensive school and teachers accustomed to streaming, operating in the context of a mixed-ability class, are obvious cases where increases in role conflict may occur. There is no suggestion made here that current educational and organisational changes are ill-considered, on the contrary many of them seem to be functional developments within the educational system, but taken together they involve a considerable increase in role diffuseness for many teachers and the consequences of this need close examination.

Questions of autonomy and confidence

The secondary-school teachers in this study were largely free from troubling experiences of role vulnerability because of the considerable professional autonomy which they enjoyed and also because they possessed a generally high sense of professional confidence. While teachers recognised that they were exposed to many different expectations as to how they should perform their role, they felt no pressure to comply with these expectations. This was true of teachers in all types of secondary school. It was clear that, in this respect, the British secondary-school teacher and the American school teacher inhabited very different professional worlds.

There was no marked sense of conflict either in relation to professional treatment. The teachers were generally satisfied with their treatment as professionals,[10] particularly in their relationships with head teachers and in their participation in decision-making in the schools. Where there was some high experience of this role conflict, it was most frequently associated with vulnerability arising out of a teacher's certificated status or out of his perception that his main subject specialism was regarded as 'marginal'.

Aspects of autonomy[11]

In an organisational and bureaucratic society, autonomy represents a safety zone for the individual—a barrier against the press of the environment and particularly against pressures towards uniformity. Moreover it provides the essential context within which an individual's need for 'self actualisation'[12] can be expressed. Given a degree of autonomy, the individual can, where appropriate, interpret the nature of a role and its activities. On the other hand, it is clear that autonomy has its limits—there are needs for co-ordination, co-operation, the specifying of particular activities, some degree of supervision and evaluation and account-ability to external agencies. The dilemma of modern society and of modern organisations is to find the right balance between these two sets of needs.

Within the work situation, Lawler (1970, p. 163) has drawn attention to the importance of autonomy as a factor in motivation and satisfaction, 'the individual must feel he has a high degree of self-control over setting his own goals and the paths to these goals.' The teacher in Britain enjoys a high degree of self-determination in his role and this autonomy serves both to protect him from the experience of serious role conflict and to provide him with a major source of satisfaction. Currently however developments are taking place which may involve a reduction in teacher autonomy. Among these are the move for more active parental involvement in schools, the growth of bureaucratic procedures and the introduction of new approaches such as team teaching and inter-disciplinary enquiry. Musgrove and Taylor (1969, p. 7) have argued that 'the freedom of teachers is the profession's glory; it is the people's shame', and have suggested that the extensive powers of teachers to determine ends as well as means within a compulsory system of education is due for modification.

Accepting that certain modifications in teacher autonomy are necessary for innovation in approaches to learning, closer community involvement and the safe-guarding of the rights of 'clients'—a serious reduction in teacher autonomy would probably be a disaster.[13] While teachers in America are seeking to reduce their exposure to conflicts of role vulnerability by establishing the need for professional autonomy, it would be ironic if teachers in Britain were to see theirs undermined. Autonomy in the teaching situation obviously cannot be allowed to obstruct all change on the grounds that 'teachers know best', but bearing in mind its important associations with motivation, satisfaction and freedom from feelings of vulnerability, it is a factor to be modified with great care.[14]

Aspects of confidence

'Teaching is largely a matter of confidence and if the system of teacher training does not create confidence either in teachers or the employers of teachers, there is something radically wrong.'[15] The General Secretary of the National Union of Teachers, in making this comment at a recent conference concerned with teacher education, has argued that colleges of education are failing to produce a sufficient sense of confidence in their students. It can be suggested that while deficiencies in the actual content and structure of preparation courses are likely to contribute towards lack of professional confidence, this study indicates that the nature of the final award is also an important factor. Graduate teachers felt confident of their professional status, although their technical preparation for teaching in terms of methodology and the study of Education was of a much shorter duration than that of certificated teachers. On the other hand, some certificated teachers felt less confident that the public accorded them professional status, despite their longer technical preparation and the fact that they were involved in demanding teaching assignments requiring a high level of professional skill.

This anomalous situation results from the fact that public recognition of professional status in teaching is determined to a large extent by graduate qualifications—which are visible—rather than by actual skilled role performance—which is generally not visible. Thus a graduate teacher who may in fact be professionally mediocre in terms of teaching skills can still repose in a sense of professional confidence arising from his graduate status—while a certificated teacher who may be an excellent and skilled practitioner feels vulnerable about his status especially in an increasingly graduate society. Fortunately, opportunities are now available for certificated teachers to study for a degree of bachelor of education during their initial training or through in-service courses and the possession of this qualification can be expected to reduce role conflicts associated with professional vulnerability. It seems desirable, for this reason, that such opportunities should be made widely available for all certificated teachers and that in the long term the profession should be totally graduate.[16]

Role conflict associated with a feeling that a teacher's main subject does not have parity of esteem with other subjects in the school may prove a more intractable problem. Cultural determinants, the views of parents and pupils, the orientation of a school, the patronage of head teachers and the attitudes of colleagues are all factors which contribute towards or prevent feelings of vulnerability arising from marginal professional status. No simple solution to such conflict can be expected. The general trend of events however does point to a steady diminution in 'status differentials' among various subjects as a result of a wider and more comprehensive concept of the educative process. Similarly, a growing realisation among some head teachers that their 'executive professional leadership' requires them to be aware of such role conflict among members of their staff, and if possible to ameliorate it, is an encouraging sign. A teacher cannot be expected to exhibit professional confidence in his dealings with parents and pupils if he feels that his head teacher regards his work as peripheral to the main business of the school. An important area of role conflict in secondary schools could be to some extent resolved if more head teachers grasped this basic fact and acted upon it.

A question of career

Role conflict arising from expectations for commitment to a school and the welfare of its pupils and the perceived realities of career advancement was generally seen by the sample to be a significant problem in the teaching situation. The majority of teachers endorsed the view that commitment by them (expressed in a given number of years service) was functional to the intellectual and social development of their pupils and to the smooth operation of schools as organisations. At the same time, they perceived a close association between rapid mobility among schools—'gaining experience'—and actual advancement in the profession. While a majority of teachers in all types of school saw this as a significant role conflict, men teachers in secondary modern schools were most affected by troubling personal experience of this conflict. It was apparent that these teachers were in a situation of high conflict, caught between pressing economic needs for career advancement on the one hand and particularly strong convictions that secondary modern school pupils needed teachers who were committed to stay at a school for a reasonable number of years. In addition to this, such teachers in this study were performing their roles within generally small schools with limited advanced work, with the result that internal career structures were limited and offered little relief for this conflict.

In an attempt to resolve these tensions many of the teachers sought to define reasonable commitment as four or five years service to a school, which could then be legitimately followed by mobility and career advancement. But even this compromise seemed unsatisfactory since there was a widespread conviction that the man who moved rapidly every two years, changing types of school, impressed interviewing committees, while the man with five years' service in one school was seen as a 'stick in the mud'. The result was a sense of betrayal, a belief that qualities of dedication and willingness to sustain a course of action counted for little and there was a bitterness over the values and priorities that were seen to operate in career advancement in teaching.[17]

The implications of these findings are not as straight-forward as they might at first seem, since they involve consideration of a number of relatively unexplored issues, but certain possibilities for action are suggested here.

The teacher's commitment

The first and most obvious need seems to be for empirical research to focus upon the relative effects of teacher continuity and teacher mobility on the actual behaviour and achievements of pupils and on the functioning of schools as organisations. It seems essential to know empirically whether or not sustained relationships with particular teachers *are* of crucial importance, especially in the education and development of pupils of average or below average ability—or what particular pattern of continuity or mobility appears most functional.[18] If such research confirms the assertions of Education Reports and the convictions of practising teachers that continuity and stability of staff is of major importance, then it is reasonable to expect a reward structure in the teaching profession which will recognise the value of the competent, committed teacher. While there will always be individual teachers who are prepared to renounce career aspirations in order to give dedicated service to their pupils, an educational system cannot operate on the assumption that this will be the norm. There will always be a continuing tension and conflict in teaching, as in other roles, between self-interest and the interests of others but present circumstances as perceived by many teachers seem to polarise these factors and to exacerbate the conflict unnecessarily.

Career patterns

It seems probable that when research is undertaken on the relative effects of teacher continuity and teacher mobility, certain advantages in terms of affective relationships with pupils will be associated with the former and certain advantages in terms of innovation and stimulus associated with the latter. Many experienced teachers and head teachers have asserted in this inquiry that a crucial problem in the functioning of schools is to get the right balance between the 'stability men' and the 'mobility men'. The problem which some schools and some teachers are facing is that existing career structures and policies appear to favour the 'mobility men'—with a consequent threat to stability and continuity of relationships in the schools. If this is the case generally (rather than just in the confines of this study), then a modification of existing career structures and policies seems necessary.

The size of schools as organisations is obviously a crucial factor in this modification. Since the small school offers only a limited internal career structure, its staff are placed in a vulnerable role conflict position. The large school, on the other hand, makes it possible for a teacher to be committed to a group of pupils without sacrificing career possibilities. Whatever doubts may be cast upon the value of the large comprehensive school in particular, from the point of view of teacher career patterns it appears to be an ideal unit. It offers suitable opportunities in its academic hierarchy for some teachers and suitable opportunities in its pastoral hierarchy for those teachers who are skilled in personal relationships and counselling. The growth of large schools containing well-structured internal career possibilities seems then, from this point of view, to be a welcome development.

The size of schools as organisations is however only one of a number of variables which are closely related to teacher career patterns. The 'policy' of various local authorities as represented in the attitudes of their education officials and appointing committees is also obviously important. But the issue which is perhaps most central and most controversial is the question of teacher effectiveness.

In an ideal meritocratic society, 'effectiveness' (reliably defined and measured) could be expected to be highly correlated with career status. Even in these circumstances however the teaching profession is likely to remain a particular problem because of the difficulty of determining and evaluating criteria of effectiveness —and of measuring certain educational outcomes. Because of this difficulty (and questions of teacher autonomy) there is a tendency to base judgments on the 'visibles'. These include the teacher's professional and academic qualifications, the success record of his pupils in external examinations, his contribution to extra-curricular activities and the positions of responsibility which he has held in various schools. Thus it is that 'variety of experience' becomes a career asset—since it carries with it implications of effectiveness—while comparatively long service in one school (which may in fact have been highly effective) makes less impact. In the absence of some reliable objective assessment of effectiveness, the teacher feels that he must be mobile in order to demonstrate that he is effective. The wider repercussions of this situation are that many teachers feel that mobility, showmanship, paper qualifications and examination cramming become the basic ingredients of career success and advancement.

If career patterns in teaching are to be tied more closely to high quality role performance then research into, and evaluation of, teacher effectiveness must be developed. Flanders (1964) has indicated the complexity of this issue and the problems which such research faces, but the need is underlined—'non-teachers have a right to expect the teaching profession to take an active part in the development of successful methods for evaluating teacher effectiveness. The mark of a true professional is an active concern for developing criteria for professional effectiveness.'

Unless some attempt is made to determine such criteria and to evaluate more systematically, effective role performance, then the career-commitment conflict of teachers seems likely to remain sharp.

A question of values

Most of the teachers in this study saw their role in a value conflict situation with undesirable tendencies in the culture. While they sought to maintain the values of honesty, truthfulness, respect for persons and property, thrift and the importance of the work-success ethic—they perceived a society in which these values were progressively losing ground. A similar sense of conflict occurred also in relation to their efforts to maintain appropriate standards of appearance and ideas of loyalty to the school.

It was the conviction of many teachers that it was their responsibility to uphold these traditional virtues in the face of 'general slackness' in society and there was a belief that the majority of parents expected such action. At the same time, there was a feeling that parents did not back up the teacher's efforts sufficiently and that teachers were, to some extent, being 'used' to make a stand on values. Teachers in all types of secondary school saw value conflict in these terms as a significant problem of the teaching situation. Teachers in secondary modern schools were once more characterised by significantly higher personal experience of such conflict. Young teachers were less troubled than their older colleagues over value conflicts. This was partly because they saw the teacher's role in more open terms, with less commitment to a particular set of values, and partly because they had less sense of a decline of standards in society. There was some indication that certain young teachers felt more value conflict with their senior colleagues in the schools than with prevailing tendencies in the culture.

These findings are hardly exceptional. It is probable that teachers in every period of history have seen themselves in value conflict with their societies and have gloried in such conflict. It is equally probable—if not certain—that older teachers have always tended to see a decline in values and standards, while their younger colleagues have seen the dawn of a better time. The context of an advanced industrial society where pluralism in values is evident presents however particularly acute problems for the teacher. These centre upon the need for clarification of the teacher's role in a changed value climate[19] and upon the nature of the teacher's education and professional preparation for dealing with value issues.

The teacher and values

The teacher will always be in a conflict situation over values since he has to contend with legitimate parental expectations, his own value commitments and his intellectual concern with the critical attitude and the pursuit of truth. There can be no permanent resolution of this conflict nor would this be desirable. However, it is possible to develop a less *ad hoc* approach to this conflict than that which exists at present. For instance, it seems desirable that parents, teachers and senior pupils should explicitly recognise value problems or conflicts and should engage in open and frank discussion of the issues. A good deal of such discussion already takes place over academic questions and career plans. It can be suggested that value issues warrant the same attention and approach rather than being left as unexamined sources of conflict in the school. The bringing together of parents, teachers and senior pupils would recognise the involvement of all in such matters and would ensure that the teacher was not left as an isolated agent caught in the crossfire of generations. In this way the teacher's role may become more clearly defined—not as the mere agent of conventional morality nor as the subversive agent of 'new' morality, but involved, in co-operation with others, in the search for a rational approach to value alternatives.[20]

Professional preparation

If teachers are to cope adequately with the value conflicts and confusions which they meet in modern secondary schools, it seems essential that their education and professional preparation should be relevant to the condition of value pluralism rather than of value consensus. In this sense the model of the teacher-missionary has to give ground to the model of the teacher-counsellor.

This inquiry indicates the need for teachers to have engaged in serious and analytical study of value problems in a pluralist society. It underlines the importance of including sociological studies in the education of teachers as an aid to developing a wider cultural perspective on values. It underlines also the importance of current courses in the philosophy of education which attempt to develop appropriate techniques of rational analysis.

The danger of the present situation is that teachers who are ill-equipped educationally and professionally to deal with value alternatives may ultimately react by making a 'firm stand' response with no room for dialogue. This can only result in greater teacher–pupil alienation in secondary schools and will demonstrate the extent of the 'cultural lag' between professional training and the realities which teachers face.

Appendix I

The role conflict schedules

Schedule I (role conflict perception)

The following statements refer to possible problems that are involved in the teacher's work. Regardless of your personal experience of these problems will you please indicate whether you see them as actual problems for teachers and if so how important you believe them to be in the teaching situation.

Scale: THIS SEEMS TO ME TO BE
      0. Not a problem at all
      1. A problem of little importance
      2. A problem of moderate importance
      3. A problem of great importance
      4. A problem of very great importance
Please enter in the box the appropriate number to indicate your reaction.

Area I: (i) Whereas many occupations give clear 'knowledge of results' to practitioners, teaching by its very nature can do this only to a limited extent.

      (ii) The teacher's work requires a considerable input of energy and yet for all this the teacher can never be certain of what he has accomplished with his pupils.

Area II: (iii) The teacher, unlike many professional practitioners, is subject to a variety of conflicting opinions as to how he should carry out his professional work.

      (iv) The teacher is a professional practitioner but despite this is generally treated as if he were not.

Area III: (v) To obtain promotion the teacher must be mobile and 'gain experience', yet the nature of the work ideally requires a sustained relationship with particular groups of pupils.

(vi) In this society which stresses 'getting on' it is becoming increasingly difficult for the teacher to stay committed to a particular school.

Area IV: (vii) The teacher is expected to maintain traditional values and standards yet at the same time society in general largely ignores these values and standards.

(viii) In a society which is becoming sceptical and permissive it is increasingly difficult for teachers to maintain traditional values and standards.

Please add further comment if you care to.

Schedule II (role conflict experience)

In the previous schedule you were asked whether you saw certain suggested problems as actual problems in the teaching situation. Will you please indicate here whether any of these problems has caused you any *personal concern* (i.e. that you have 'felt' this problem and been to some extent troubled by it). If so, will you please indicate to what extent.

Scale: I HAVE PERSONALLY FELT THIS AS A PROBLEM
   0. Not at all
   1. To a small extent
   2. To a moderate extent
   3. To a great extent
   4. To a very great extent

Please enter in the box the appropriate number to indicate your reaction.

Items of schedule I repeated here.

Appendix II

Teacher interviews

Section A: Role diffuseness

A -1 (high scorers) Your score indicated that you saw 'knowledge of results'—knowing what you had accomplished with your pupils—as being an important problem in teaching. Could you tell me something more about this?

A - 2 (low scorers) Your score indicated that 'knowledge of results' —knowing what you had accomplished—was not an important problem for you. Could you give me further details on this? In what ways does the teacher receive feedback of the results of his efforts?

A - 3 (all) Has your sense of achievement—of what you have accomplished with your pupils—been affected in any way by the introduction of 'new' approaches in teaching e.g. 'new' maths, Nuffield science, IDE, etc.?

Section B: Role vulnerability

B - 1 (high scorers —item iii) Your score indicated that you found the many conflicting opinions about the nature of teaching to be an important problem. Can you tell me in what way this is so?

B - 2 (low scorers —item iii) Your score on this item was low—is this because you don't accept that there are many conflicting opinions about the nature of teaching or because these opinions don't trouble you?

B - 3 (high scorers — item iv)	Your score suggested that you see an important problem in the lack of professional treatment for teachers. Can you tell me what particular agency is in your view responsible for this lack of proper professional treatment, e.g. 'the general public', head teachers, the l.e.a., inspectors, etc.?
B - 4 (low scorers —item iv)	Your score suggested that you saw no major problem about appropriate professional treatment for teachers. Could you give me further details on this? Are you generally satisfied with your treatment as a professional?
B - 5 (all)	Do you feel satisfied with the amount of involvement which you have in decision-making in the school?

Section C: Role commitment v. career orientation

C - 1 (high scorers)	Your score indicated that you saw an important problem in teaching between the demands of commitment and the demands of career. Could you tell me something more about this?
C - 2 (low scorers)	You did not see conflict between commitment and career as a particular problem in teaching. Could you give me further details on this?

Section D: Values

D - 1 (high scorers)	Your score indicated that you saw an important problem in the teaching situation in trying to maintain certain values and standards in the climate of modern society. Could you tell me something more about this?
D - 2 (high scorers)	Could you tell me which particular values and standards you see as being most 'at risk' in present circumstances?
D - 3 (low scorers)	You did not see a major problem in this area. Is this because you don't accept the view of the teacher as the upholder of traditional values—or because you don't see any major conflict between 'school values' and 'society values'?

Head teacher interviews: Section A—Recognition functions

A - 1   Do you see it as part of your role to provide some form of verbal recognition for staff effort—or do you regard this as more of the province of the appropriate head of department—or—

A - 2   Do you take the view that mature professional persons don't need this sort of recognition?

Section B—Professional leadership functions

B - 1   Do you take the view that what is taught and the mode of teaching is essentially the affair of the individual teacher or subject department—or do you feel that it is part of your function to encourage the selection of certain material or the adoption of certain teaching methods?

B - 2   What action would you take if you felt dissatisfied with the selection of material or approaches of a particular teacher or even of a particular department?

B - 3   To what extent does the head teacher need staff support before introducing broad changes in school policy which he feels are essential?

Section C—Commitment and career

C - 1   Some people feel that teachers ought to be committed to a particular school and groups of pupils for a reasonable period of time (4/5 years). Others claim that promotion and salary increases go to those who move frequently, gaining 'variety of experience'.

       To what extent do the factors of commitment on the one hand and variety of experience on the other influence you when you are making an appointment or allocating an allowance?

C - 2   Do you feel that commitment to a school is important—and how do you define commitment?

Section D—Values

D - 1   Do you see it as part of the role of the head teacher and of assistant teachers to maintain traditional values and standards (traditional morality, honesty, respect for persons and property, thrift and working hard for success) in the face of growing scepticism?

D - 2   If a member of your staff did not subscribe to one or more of these value commitments and this was known to the pupils (as a result of the frank answering of questions)—do you feel that you would have any responsibility to intervene?

Appendix III

a   The sample

Characteristics of the sample compared with characteristics of the
secondary school teaching population in maintained schools in England
and Wales as at 31 March 1967.

Characteristics	The sample (150)		National population (150,803)	
	n	%	n	%
Men	87	58	88,942	59
Women	63	42	61,861	41
Modern school	69	46	69,942	46.3
Grammar school	43	28.7	38,595	25.6
Bilateral school	38	25.3	n.a.	n.a.
Age: under 40	101	67.3	88,719	58.9
Age: 40 - 59	44	29.3	55,591	36.8
Age: 60+	5	3.3	5,409	4.3
Graduate	80	53.3	59,959	39.8
Certificated	70	46.7	89,760	60.2

b   The interview sub-sample

Characteristics	$n = 80$
Men	47
Women	33
S. modern	40
Bilateral	19
Grammar	21
Age: under 40	44
Age: 40 - 59	33
Age: 60+	3
Graduate	39
Certificated	41
High scorers (overall) RCP	38
Low scorers (overall) RCP	42

Notes

Introduction

1 Willard Waller, *The Sociology of Teaching*, p. 457.
2 Aaron V. Cicourel, *Method and Measurement in Sociology*, p. 20.
3 Waller, op cit., preface.

Chapter 1   Approaches to the study of role conflict

1 R. L. Kahn *et al.*, *Organizational Stress: Studies in Role Conflict and Ambiguity*, p. 19.
2 M. Seeman, 'Role conflict and ambivalence in leadership', *Am. Soc. Rev.*, XVIII (1953), p. 373.
3 See W. Charters, 'The social background of teaching' in N. Gage (ed.), *Handbook of Research on Teaching*, p. 795: 'The problem of role conflict is a different one from the problem of role agreement and disagreement.' See also L. J. Westwood, 'The role of the teacher—II', *Educ. Research*, X (1) (1967), p. 33: 'The naive assumption that all lack of consensus leads to conflict.'
4 T. R. Sarbin, 'Role theory' in Lindzey, G. (ed.), *Handbook of Social Psychology*, p. 228.
5 For a review of the literature on conflicts of professionals in bureaucratic organisations, see P. M. Blau and W. R. Scott, *Formal Organizations: A Comparative Approach*.
6 See Charters, op. cit.
7 R. K. Merton, *Social Theory and Social Structure*, Free Press, 1957, p. 369.
8 N. Gross, W. S. Mason and A. W. McEachern, *Explorations in Role Analysis*, p. 248.

9 The position of the student teacher is especially vulnerable to role conflict. The student is at the focal point of two powerful sets of expectations—those from the college or department of education, mediated through the tutors, and those from the 'practice school', mediated through the teachers and head teacher. When these expectations conflict, the student is in an unenviable position. The resolution of this conflict by students illustrates the strategies discussed later in the chapter, e.g.—retreat into cynicism, playing one group off against the other or elaborate compromise, ensuring that the right 'performance' is presented for the right person. The role conflicts of student teachers justify a research project in themselves!

10 The term 'cognitive dissonance' is sometimes used to describe this situation—see L. Festinger, *A Theory of Cognitive Dissonance.*

11 E. G. Guba and C. E. Bidwell, *Administrative Relationships,* p. 8.

12 J. W. Getzels, 'Conflict and role behaviour in the educational setting' in W. Charters and N. Gage (eds), *Readings in the Social Psychology of Education,* p. 318.

13 See D. Rugh, 'The American teacher—victim of role inflation', *J. Teacher Educ.* See also G. H. Bantock, 'Conflicts of values in teacher education' in W. Taylor (ed.), *Towards a Policy for the Education of Teachers,* pp. 122-34. Bantock analyses the dangers of 'global pretensions' for the teacher's role.

14 J. W. Getzels and E. G. Guba, 'Role, role conflict and effectiveness: an empirical study', *Am. Soc. Rev.,* XIX, p. 173.

15 J. Toby, 'Some variables in role conflict analysis', *Social Forces,* XXX, p. 327.

16 For a recent, strong statement of this view, see Christopher Price's article, 'A medal for Mrs. Clarkson', *The Times Educational Supplement,* 21 January 1971.

17 L. Coser, *The Functions of Social Conflict,* p. 154.

18 Kahn *et al., op. cit.,* p. 53.

19 Charters, *op. cit.,* p. 748.

Chapter 2   The teacher and role conflict

1 The emphasis here is upon the role conflicts of secondary-school teachers.

2 Kahn *et al., Organizational Stress: Studies in Role Conflict and Ambiguity,* p. 73, distinguish between 'role conflict' and 'role ambiguity'. Role ambiguity is defined as: 'a direct function of the discrepancy

between the information available to a person and that which is required for adequate performance of his role. Subjectively, it is the difference between his actual state of knowledge and that which would provide adequate satisfaction of his personal needs and values.' In the present study, role ambiguity is taken to be a situation of potential self-role conflict.

3 Quoted in L. Spolton, 'D. H. Lawrence: student and teacher', *Brit. J. educ. Studies*, XIV (3), 1965-6, p. 31.

4 A. S. Neill, *The Problem Teacher*, p. 47.

5 J. E. Gerstl, 'Education and the sociology of work' in Hanson, D. and Gerstl, J., *On Education: Sociological Perspectives*, p. 247.

6 See M. B. Miles, 'Planned change and organizational health' in Carver, F. and Sergiovanni, T., *Organizations and Human Behavior: Focus on Schools*, p. 383. It should be noted, however, that Miles was sceptical about these reactions which he regarded as 'defensive solutions to the actual problems of goal ambiguity' (p. 383).

7 B. R. Wilson, 'The teacher's role: a sociological analysis', *Brit. J. Sociol.*, XIII (1), p. 28.

8 Ibid.

9 R. K. Merton, 'The role-set: problems in sociological theory', *Brit. J. Sociol.*, VIII (2), p. 112.

10 F. Musgrove and P. H. Taylor, 'Teachers' and parents' conception of the teacher's role', *Brit. J. Educ. Psychol.*, XXXV (2), p. 178.

11 Musgrove and Taylor, *Society and the Teacher's Role*, p. 54.

12 Op. cit., p. 29.

13 Recent work in the sociology of the school (Hargreaves 1967; King 1969; Lacey 1970) has focused upon processes of 'sub-cultural polarization' taking place among pupils, related to the question of streaming. There has been little reference to teacher roles or role conflicts in these studies. For a study which does relate aspects of organisational change and teacher role conflicts, see C. M. Turner, 'An organisational analysis of a secondary modern school', *Soc. Rev.*, XVII (1).

14 R. G. Corwin, *A Sociology of Education*, p. 217.

15 Not all teachers have a 'professional orientation'. See Corwin's distinction between 'professional' and 'employee' roles.

16 For a study which questions this, see G. Moeller and W. Charters, 'Relation of Bureaucratization to sense of power among teachers' in Carver and Sergiovanni, op. cit., p. 235.

17 Musgrove and Taylor, op. cit., 1969, p. 79.

18 Op. cit., p. 30.

19 Ibid., p. 26.

20 Ibid., p.31.
21 J. Floud, 'Teaching in the affluent society', *Brit. J. Sociol.* XIII, p. 301.
22 An unbelievable amount of conflict in schools occurs over questions of appropriate dress and appearance. Such conflict occurs not only in relation to the pupils but also in relation to young teachers and student teachers. Conflict can arise over long hair, jeans, coloured socks, ear-rings, high boots, long skirts and short skirts, or any form of dress seen to be 'bizarre'.
23 R. A. King, *Values and Involvement in a Grammar School*, p. 70.
24 Considerable interest has been shown in America, in value differences of teachers and pupils related to social class but even here Charters (op. cit.) concludes that work has been more in the realm of hypothesis than of empirical investigation.
25 Op. cit., p. 28.
26 An important area yet to be explored is the potential role conflict situation created by continuous assessment procedures and by the move away from externally marked examinations. A teacher's knowledge of how hard a pupil has worked and the general context of affective relationships may provoke a difficult situation when the teacher has to attempt an objective assessment of the quality of the work.

Chapter 3   Present perspectives

1 The use of the word 'results' in (item i) was unfortunate, since it is a word with strong emotive associations in the teaching profession, dating back to the days of 'payment by results'. The neutral term 'outcomes' would have been preferable.
2 Inter-item correlation in the role vulnerability area was at an acceptable level. Schedule I Φ = 0.48 p = <0.01; Schedule II Φ = 0.52 p = <0.01.
3 The distribution of the schedules at group meetings in the schools gave an opportunity to clarify this item more exactly, i.e. 'maintain' —to uphold to the pupils (not necessarily in the teacher's private life).
'traditional values and standards'—honesty, truthfulness, Christian morality, respect for persons and property, thrift, belief in the value of hard work.
4 This seemed to produce a generally co-operative attitude towards the research. Teachers in some schools asked for a report back of

129

the findings and this was subsequently done. Many teachers complained that they were too often 'used' for research without being notified of any findings.

5 With two items in each role conflict area, scores were in the range 0 - 8. These were arbitrarily dichotomised and scores of 0 - 4 were classified as 'low' and scores of 5 - 8 were classified as 'high'. The purpose here was to focus the scores in terms of 'high' scores and others (referred to as 'low').

6 An overall score was taken to be 'high' if the mean score for each role conflict area was in the range 5 - 8. Thus overall scores were arbitrarily dichotomised and scores of 20 - 32 were classified as 'high' and scores of 0 - 19 as 'low'.

7 Comparisons using groups based on main subject specialism were used only for overall RCP and RCE scores.

8 The classification of schools was based on the researcher's local knowledge and upon information supplied by the head teachers. Comparisons using groups based on the social class composition of the schools were used only for overall RCP and RCE scores and not for individual role conflict areas.

9 See R. K. Merton, M. Fiske and P. L. Kendall, *The Focussed Interview*.

10 The interview sub-sample was necessarily self-selected but every effort was made to ensure that it was as representative of the total sample as possible. See Appendix III.

11 Extending over a period of six years and involving regular contact with most of the schools.

12 Although officially styled 'bilateral' (grammar/modern) these schools are in fact run largely as comprehensives.

13 Within the county, these schools are referred to as 'high schools' and most of them offer extended courses leading to external examinations. In this study they are referred to by the more usual name of secondary modern schools.

14 Information supplied by the Department of Education and Science. See Appendix III.

Chapter 4   Perceptions and experiences

1 No significant differences in overall RCP scores were found between men and women teachers; teachers in various subject groupings; grammar and bilateral schools teachers or teachers in schools of different social class composition.

2 No significant differences in overall RCE scores were found between teachers in various subject groupings; more experienced and less experienced teachers; grammar and bilateral school teachers or secondary modern and bilateral school teachers.

3 Teachers of more than ten years experience saw significantly more conflict than did teachers of less than ten years experience ($\chi^2 = 7.16$ d.f. $= 1$ $p < 0.01$).
When teachers were divided into three experience categories (a. 0 - 9 years: b. 10 - 19 years: c. 20 + years) the proportion having high RCP scores increased steadily (a. 34.9%: b. 47.4%: c. 65.5%) but differences reached significance only in the comparison of group a. with group c ($\chi^2 = 8.28$ d.f. $= 1$ $p < 0.01$).

4 It must be emphasised that this refers to overall levels of role conflict. A significant difference in role conflict experience was apparent in the value conflict area. See Chapter 8.

5 Adaptation over time to role conflict in the teaching situation is an important subject in need of further research. 'Dysfunctional' adaptations by teachers may result in a less efficient learning environment.

6 Within the bilateral schools, 29.6 per cent of graduates had high RCP scores compared with 45.5 per cent of certificated teachers ($\chi^2 = 0.28$ d.f. $= 1$ n.s.).
Within the secondary modern schools, 38.8 per cent of graduates had high scores compared with 62.7 per cent of certificated teachers ($\chi^2 = 2.23$ d.f. $= 1$ n.s.).

7 44.3 per cent of certificated teachers had high RCP scores in the role diffuseness area compared with 27.5 per cent of graduates ($\chi^2 = 4.72$ d.f. $= 1$ p < 0.05).
30 per cent of certificated teachers had high RCE scores in this area compared with 15 per cent of graduates ($\chi^2 = 4.89$ d.f. $= 1$ p < 0.05).

8 63.7 per cent of secondary modern teachers had high RCP scores in the role vulnerability area compared with 42.1 per cent of bilateral-school teachers ($\chi^2 = 4.66$ d.f. $= 1$ p <0.05)—and 25.6 per cent of grammar-school teachers ($\chi^2 = 15.4$ d.f. $= 1$ p <0.01).

9 See Chapters 5 and 6.

10 This is not to suggest that women teachers are less conscientious than men but it is likely that cultural influences make for higher achievement orientation and role identification among men than among women.

11 77 per cent of the men teachers in secondary modern schools were certificated.

12 See R. Rosenthal and L. Jacobson, *Pygmalion in the Classroom: teacher expectation and pupils' intellectual development,* Holt, Rinehart & Winston, 1968.

Chapter 5 Diffuseness and conflict

1 The two bilateral schools represented opposite ends of the educational continuum. One school was strongly oriented towards examination goals, while the other was a pioneer in the area for inter-disciplinary approaches to learning, where examinations were only one of a number of goals thought to be important.

The majority of the men bilateral-school teachers were in an atmosphere which was particularly 'specific' and goal oriented, while the women were in an atmosphere which was unusually 'diffuse' for the area. These specific situational factors clearly affected the pattern of scores which had emerged in comparisons in the secondary modern and grammar schools.

2 This has been recognised by those advocating new approaches to teaching and learning. See *Forum,* 13(2), 1971, p. 39: 'Teachers are particularly vulnerable in flexible teaching/learning environments; they "give out" in such a variety of ways that it becomes easy to underestimate achievement.' The current attention being given to problems of assessment and evaluation in education is partly a response to this situation.

3 The feelings expressed by this grammar-school master reflect exactly the points made by Floud, 'Teaching in the affluent society', *Brit. J. Sociol.,* XIII, p. 304, on the growth of 'a utilitarian, more or less cynical attitude towards what the teacher has to offer—an emphasis on instruction and know-how'.

4 For a review of the effects of size of organisations upon their personnel, see R. G. Barker and P. V. Gump, *Big School, Small School,* pp. 29-37. Wilson (1962, p. 29) believes that the growth in the size of schools 'makes more difficult the affective elements of the teacher's role.'

5 See A. Cohen, E. Scotland and D. Wolfe, 'An experimental investigation of need for cognition', *J. abnorm. soc. Psychol.* (51), 1955, pp. 291-4.

6 One teacher suggested that the cynicism of older teachers was more apparent than real—a protective adaptation to the strains and disappointments of the work. It might not be a true indicator of their attitudes or behaviour.

Chapter 6   Vulnerability and conflict

1 20.4 per cent of teachers in the twenty to twenty-nine age group had high RCE scores on this item compared with 17 per cent in the 30 to 39 age group, 16.7 per cent in the 40 to 49 group and 25 per cent in the 50 to 59 group. There were no significant differences in these comparisons.

2 Important relationships between amount of autonomy/self-determination and job satisfaction have been suggested in a number of studies. See for example N. C. Morse and E. Reimer, 'The experimental change of a major organization variable', *J. abnorm. soc. Psychol.* (52), 1956, pp. 120-9. A recent British study investigating the role conflicts and role strain of scientists in industrial laboratories found that, 'by far the largest single source of strain reported, centred around the problem of autonomy'. See S. Cotgrove and S. Box, *Science, Industry and Society: Studies in the Sociology of Science,* p. 98.

3 Eyre & Spottiswoode, 1963, p. 233.

4 Men teachers were particularly conscious of this and there were bitter comments that teaching would never become a true profession until 'standards' were raised. 'We must make it a worthwhile thing to do', and 'there is too much rubbish in the teaching profession' were typical comments.

5 Musgrove and Taylor, *Society and the Teacher's Role,* p. 15, suggest a tendency among teachers to refer to 'a golden age of teaching which in fact never existed.'

6 Kahn *et al., Organizational Stress: Studies in Role Conflict and Ambiguity,* p. 86, discuss the importance of evaluations by colleagues.

7 The caretaker is a not inconsiderable power in the school. A wry joke among school teachers is that a serious conflict between the caretaker and an assistant teacher is more likely to result in the latter leaving the school rather than the former. Waller, as always, was aware of the realities of school life— 'The janitor has, it is true, a very limited theoretical status but his actual influence is often out of proportion to this theoretical place in the school system.' W. Waller, *The Sociology of Teaching,* p. 80.

Chapter 7   Commitment and conflict

1 The career structures in the secondary modern school study were limited because of the small size of the organisations and the restricted amount of advanced work which they could undertake.

2 The 'local' orientation of certificated teachers (expressed in choice of work area) has been shown in a number of studies. See L. J. Jay, 'The mobility of teachers'. See also E. P. Duggan and W. A. C. Stewart, 'The choice of work area of teachers', *The Sociological Review Monograph 15.*

3 It has been suggested that the supervision of student teachers in schools should be undertaken by experienced and successful serving teachers who would be styled 'master teachers'. At present, the main responsibility for this supervision lies with visiting tutors and this system has been criticised on the grounds of inefficiency and expense. See R. Pedley, 'Teacher training: a new approach', *Education,* 4 June 1965.

4 The pervasive idea of 'teaching as a vocation' has embodied an implicit rejection of 'career thinking' for teachers. For some teachers, a career orientation is inconsistent with the values which the teacher is expected to embody and yet, as Wilson points out, the teacher is expected to encourage his pupils to have a career orientation.

5 The implications for the teacher's role and career structure of developments in higher education are discussed in G. Bernbaum, 'Educational expansion and the teacher's role', *Universities Quarterly,* March 1967.

6 O. Grusky, 'The effects of succession: a comparative study of military and business organisation' in O. Grusky and G. Miller, *The Sociology of Organizations: Basic Studies,* p. 441.

7 The idea that the short-stay teacher 'takes more than he gives' may be a myth. The work of Grusky (op. cit.) has interesting implications. He found that short-stay personnel integrated themselves rapidly in community life. The same phenomenon may apply in the case of teachers, although the question of the importance of sustained relationships still remains.

8 This practice in itself can cause further difficulties. The head who rewards loyalty and commitment with responsibility allowances may alienate young teachers who believe that merit rather than loyalty should be rewarded.

Chapter 8   Values and conflict

1 Floud, 'Teaching in the affluent society', *Brit. J. Sociol.,* XIII, p. 304, has suggested that the affluent society needs teacher/ crusaders 'dedicated to the war against mediocrity and to the search for excellence.' See also D. Riesman, 'Teachers as a counter-cyclical

influence', *Sch. Review* (65). Although Riesman is concerned here specifically with trends in education, the counter-cyclical concept clearly has wider implications.

2 'Among teachers at the secondary stage, as at the primary, moral training took pride of place over "instruction" for all except men teaching in grammar schools, who seemed to perceive their job primarily in intellectual terms.' Musgrove and Taylor, *Society and the Teacher's Role*, p. 63.

3 The concept of 'respect' is open to a number of interpretations. Most of the teachers who referred to it used it in what may be called its formal sense, i.e. regard for persons having a particular status and regard as expressed through a particular code of good manners.

4 The decline in respect for institutional authority noted by Floud and others increases the possibility of role strain for the secondary school teacher. The teacher's authority has to be found increasingly in qualities of the person rather than in the role as such. Teachers in schools in metropolitan areas would be likely to meet much more conflict than the teachers in this small town setting.

5 Older teachers are acquainted with situations where the stock-room in a school has been comparable with the strong-room in the bank and where withdrawal of resources has been just as difficult.

6 While this conflict was most frequently mentioned by secondary modern school teachers, there were a number of references to it by grammar and bilateral school teachers who felt that certain trends in society were encouraging senior pupils to expect 'instant success' in their studies.

7 There was evidence that problems of sexual morality were discussed frankly between girls and their (young) P.E. teachers. These discussions could result in difficult conflict situations for young teachers when trying to give responsible advice without appearing 'old fashioned' or naive.

8 Clashes between teachers' expectations for loyalty to the school and the local loyalties of working-class pupils in grammar schools, were found by Jackson and Marsden to be important sources of conflict. See B. Jackson and D. Marsden, *Education and the Working Class*, pp. 103-12.

9 Perhaps the most surprising finding in this area was that very few teachers referred to any personal conflict over values as a factor making for difficulties in their role. It may be however that there was an unwillingness to discuss personal value conflicts with an interviewer.

Chapter 9   The head teachers

1 See 'Subordinates as observers of a superordinate's behaviour', Appendix D in N. Gross and R. E. Herriott, *Staff Leadership in Public Schools*.

2 It is interesting that some of these head teachers felt the need for some recognition themselves and made the point that no one gave encouragement to head teachers.

3 This suggests that teacher and head teacher expectations in these schools were in agreement on this issue.

4 The majority of the head teachers saw themselves as having a responsibility to be 'agents of change' within the school. They emphasised, however, that no change of policy could hope to succeed unless the co-operation of most heads of department and senior teachers was ensured. The strategy of the head teacher was therefore to win over such individuals to a particular idea or to suggest that a change (e.g. mixed ability classes) might be introduced as an 'experiment'—to be reviewed after one or two years.

5 Such a role concept was essentially a continuation of elementary school traditions in a modern secondary school. As such it was resented and opposed by young specialist teachers in the school who regarded it as 'interfering' and 'amateur'.

6 Such slight evidence as existed of teacher dissatisfaction over professional treatment was located in the schools of the 'positive interventionists'.

7 Some heads clearly felt the need for more discretionary powers in this area. The interviewer was *asked* by a very experienced head teacher, 'How do you get rid of an incompetent teacher?'

8 The question was posed in terms of pupils having asked the teacher about his beliefs, rather than the teacher having volunteered them. The difficulties in practice of distinguishing between situations involving frank answers to questions and situations involving covert attempts at indoctrination are considerable—and the head teachers felt this to be one of their most difficult responsibilities.

9 These expectations were particularly specific in the case of the two church schools.

10 It must be emphasised that interviews followed the prescribed form and no questions were asked about a teacher's religious or political views. Head teachers made their judgments from an overall impression.

11 It is likely that students holding strong 'emergent' values will not be attracted to the role of school teacher. Those who are, may find

themselves 'cooled out' during the course of professional preparation. In this way, a good deal of value consensus is maintained in the schools.

Chapter 10 Conclusions and implications

1 The use of the term 'recognition' throughout this section implies an individual's knowledge that his efforts in role performance have been noted and that he is seen to be doing a good job.
2 While accepting that teachers have different standards of academic and professional competence which fit them to specialise at different levels within a school, it seems desirable that all teachers should have the opportunity (subject to competence) of dealing with a wide range of ability, so that the sheer chances of response and satisfying results are more equitably shared. At the moment, secondary modern teachers seem to bear the brunt of role (diffuseness) conflict, while their grammar-school colleagues live in a virtually conflict-free world.
3 The same conclusion was reached by Hargreaves:
'None of the teachers feels under the same pressure to motivate or stimulate the low stream pupils because the lack of an external examination as a goal means that there is no way in which their achievements can be externally checked. This problem is most acute for those teachers who devote the majority or all of their timetable to the low streams. They have neither the satisfaction of preparing high stream boys for the exams nor have they a measure of their own competence and effort through the externally assessed examination results. These teachers of low streams may, like their pupils, feel status deprived. Their motivation to strive must be entirely self-induced.' (*Social Relations in a Secondary School*, p. 186.)
4 Student teachers who have encountered these attitudes have been known to ask their tutors, 'Will I become like that?' It is easy of course for students and tutors as occasional visitors to the schools to maintain an attitude of bright optimism—it is quite another thing to sustain it over the years while in 'the front line'.
5 This may not always be the case. Turner noted, in his analysis of a secondary modern school ('An organisational analysis of a secondary modern school', *Soc. Rev.,* XVII (1), p. 77), that although the headmaster gave lavish praise to his staff, 'this was felt not to be based on accurate knowledge and was therefore not acceptable in terms of social exchange.'

137

6 During the interviews with head teachers it became apparent that they had many techniques for evaluating staff without involving necessarily any direct observation of actual teaching. Important among these indirect methods were the head teacher's assessment of the 'atmosphere' in classes as he 'went about the school', spontaneous comment from pupils and parents, the incidence of disciplinary problems and the head teacher's observation of a teacher's efforts beyond the normal call of duty, e.g. giving tuition in his own time, participating in extra-curricular activities, etc. Additionally, they received formal feedback from heads of department.

7 The ideas advanced by Trist seem particularly appropriate here. See E. Trist, 'The professional facilitation of planned change in organisations' in V. H. Vroom and E. L. Decci, *Management and Motivation*.

8 E. E. Lawler, 'Job design and employee motivation' in Vroom and Decci, op. cit.

9 The relationship between knowledge of results and motivation is stressed by Katz and Kahn, *The Social Psychology of Organizations*, p. 421: 'Knowledge of results can in itself motivate people toward improving their performance. Level of aspiration studies indicate that individuals tend to raise their sights when they see the outcome of their efforts. If there is continuous feedback on the basis of some objective criterion of behaviour, people will be motivated...'

10 An exception to this, for men teachers, was that current salaries were not thought to be appropriate for the professional responsibilities of teaching.

11 For an important discussion of professional autonomy in teaching see M. Lieberman, *Education as a Profession*, pp. 87-123.

12 Self-actualization—'what a man can be, he must be', is seen by Maslow as a higher order need. See A. H. Maslow, 'A theory of human motivation', *Psychol. Review*, 50.

13 This might be particularly true of recruitment to teaching. It is probable that autonomy is one of the most attractive features of the teaching profession to potential entrants.

14 If more objective attempts are made to assess teacher effectiveness some modification of existing teacher autonomy seems inevitable.

15 E. Britton 'The teaching profession and the education of teachers' in Taylor, W. (ed.), *Towards a Policy for the Education of Teachers*, p. 181.

16 The idea of an all graduate teaching profession presupposes radical changes in the present structure of the B.Ed. degree. Many teachers

feel that 'professional' work is under-represented and 'academic' work is over-represented in existing degree courses.

17 Since there is little reliable information at present about teacher career patterns it is possible that the idea that rapid movers are promoted whereas 'committed' men are passed over is a myth, or at least is true only in specific local areas. In other words, there may be a fairly general misperception of career realities in teaching. Research into actual career patterns would serve the useful practical purpose of either correcting the perceptions or making clear which areas were 'commitment rewarding' and which 'mobility rewarding'.

18 Type and rate of teacher turnover have to be specified. Many teachers claim that classes become troublesome and unsettled as the result of high teacher turnover and that this has inevitable and undesirable effects on educational attainment.
The Plowden Report however found that in primary schools, staff turnover was not in itself related to the average attainments of pupils. See Central Advisory Council for Education (England), *Children and their Primary Schools* (Plowden Report).

19 This need has been recognised in the recent literature of the Humanities Curriculum Project, Nuffield Foundation and in the publications of the Farmington Trust, Oxford.

20 For a more detailed treatment of the issues and possible courses of action see J. Wilson, N. Williams and B. Sugarman, *Introduction to Moral Education*.

Bibliography

BACCHUS, M. K. (1967), 'Some factors influencing the views of secondary modern school teachers on their pupils' interests and abilities', *Educ. Research*, 9(2), pp. 147-50.

BANTOCK, G. H. (1969), 'Conflicts of values in teacher education' in Taylor, W. (ed.), *Towards a Policy for the Education of Teachers*. Butterworths.

BARKER, R. G. and GUMP, P. V. (1964), *Big School, Small School*, Stanford University Press.

BARON, G. and TROPP, A. (1961), 'Teachers in England and America' in Halsey, A. H. *et al.* (eds), *Education, Economy and Society*, Free Press.

BECKER, H. S. (1952a), 'Social class variations in the teacher-pupil relationship', *J. educ. Sociol.*, 25, pp. 451-65.

BECKER, H. S. (1952b), 'The career of the Chicago Public Schoolteacher', *Am. J. Sociol.*, LVII, pp. 470-7.

BEN-DAVID, J. (1958), 'The professional role of the physician in bureaucratized medicine: a study in role conflict', *Human Relations*, XI(3), p. 255.

BENNIS, W. G. (1958), 'Reference Groups and Loyalties in the Out-Patient Department', *Administrative Science Quarterly*, 2, pp. 481-500.

BERNBAUM, G. (1967), 'Educational expansion and the teacher's role', *Universities Quarterly*, March, pp. 152-66.

BERNSTEIN, B. (1961), 'Social class and linguistic development: a theory of social learning' in Halsey, A. H. *et al.* (eds), *Education, Economy and Society*, Free Press.

BIDDLE, B. J. and ELLENA, W. J. (eds) (1964), *Contemporary Research on Teacher Effectiveness*, Holt, Rinehart & Winston.

BIDDLE, B. J. and THOMAS, E. (eds) (1966), *Role Theory: Concepts and Research*, Wiley.

BLAU, P. M. and SCOTT, W. R. (1963), *Formal Organizations: A Comparative Approach*, Routledge & Kegan Paul.

BOYAN, N. J. (1969), 'The emergent role of the teacher in the authority structure of the school' in Carver, F. and Sergiovanni, T. (eds), *Organisations and Human Behaviour: Focus on Schools*, McGraw-Hill.

BUCKLEY, W. (1967), *Sociology and Modern Systems Theory*, Prentice-Hall.

BURCHARD, W. (1954), 'Role conflict of military chaplains', *Amer. Sociol. Rev.*, 19, pp. 528-35.

BURNHAM, P. S. (1964), 'The role of the deputy head in secondary schools', Unpublished M.Ed. thesis, University of Leicester.

CANNON, C. (1964), 'Some variations in the teacher's role', *Education for Teaching*, May, pp. 29-36.

CAPLOW, T. and MCGEE, R. J. (1958), *The Academic Marketplace*, Basic Books.

CARVER, F. and SERGIOVANNI, T. (1969), *Organizations and Human Behavior: Focus on Schools*, McGraw-Hill.

CENTRAL ADVISORY COUNCIL FOR EDUCATION (ENGLAND) (1963), *Half Our Future*, Newsom Report, HMSO.

CENTRAL ADVISORY COUNCIL FOR EDUCATION (ENGLAND) (1967), *Children and their Primary Schools*, Plowden Report, HMSO.

CHARTERS, W. W. (1963), 'The social background of teaching' in Gage, N. (ed.), *Handbook of Research on Teaching*, Rand McNally.

CICOUREL, A. V. (1964), *Method and Measurement in Sociology*, Free Press.

CORWIN, R. G. (1965), *A Sociology of Education*, Appleton-Century-Crofts.

COSER, L. (1956), *The Functions of Social Conflict*, Routledge & Kegan Paul.

COTGROVE, S. and BOX, S. (1970), *Science, Industry and Society: Studies in the Sociology of Science*, Allen & Unwin.

CRAFT, M. (1967), 'The Teacher/social worker' in Craft, M. *et al.* (eds), *Linking Home and School*, Longmans.

DUGGAN, E. P. and STEWART, W. A. C. (1970), 'The choice of work area of teachers', *The Sociological Review Monograph 15*, Keele University.

FESTINGER, L. (1957), *A Theory of Cognitive Dissonance*, Harper & Row.

FLANDERS, N. A. (1964), 'Teacher influence, pupil attitudes and achievement' in B. J. Biddle and W. J. Ellena (eds), *Contemporary Research on Teacher Effectiveness*, p. 231.

FLOUD, J. (1962), 'Teaching in the affluent society', *Brit. J. Sociol.*, XIII, pp. 299-307.

GAGE, N. (ed.) (1963), *Handbook of Research on Teaching*, Rand McNally.

BIBLIOGRAPHY

GERSTL, J. E. (1967), 'Education and the sociology of work' in Hanson, D. and Gerstl, J. (eds), *On Education: Sociological Perspectives*, Wiley.

GETZELS, J. W. (1963), 'Conflict and role behaviour in the educational setting' in Charters, W. and Gage, N. (eds), *Readings in the Social Psychology of Education*, Alleyn and Bacon.

GETZELS, J. W. and GUBA, E. G. (1954), 'Role, role conflict and effectiveness: an empirical study', *Am. Soc. Rev.*, XIX, pp. 164-75.

GETZELS, J. W. and GUBA, E. G. (1955), 'The structure of roles and role conflicts in the teaching situation', *J. educ. Sociol.*, 29(1), pp. 30-9.

GETZELS, J. W. and GUBA, E. G. (1957), 'Social behaviour and the administrative process', *Sch. Review*, 65, pp. 423-41.

GOODE, W. J. (1960), 'A theory of role strain', *Am. Soc. Rev.*, 25, pp. 483-96.

GOULDNER, A. W. (1958), 'Cosmopolitans and locals: towards an analysis of latent social roles', *Administrative Science Quarterly*, 2, pp. 281-306.

GROSS, N. and HERRIOTT, R. E. (1965), *Staff Leadership in Public Schools*, Wiley.

GROSS, N., MASON, W. S. and MCEACHERN, A. W. (1958), *Explorations in Role Analysis: Studies of the School Superintendency Role*, Wiley.

GRUSKY, O. (1970), 'The effects of succession: a comparative study of military and business organization' in Grusky, O. and Miller, G., *The Sociology of Organizations: Basic Studies*, Free Press.

GUBA, E. G. and BIDWELL, C. E. (1957), *Administrative Relationships*, University of Chicago Press.

HALPIN, A. W. (1966), *Theory and Research in Administration*, Macmillan (N.Y.).

HANSON, D. and GERSTL, J. (1967), *On Education: Sociological Perspectives*, Wiley.

HARGREAVES, D. H. (1967), *Social Relations in a Secondary School*, Routledge & Kegan Paul.

HERRIOTT, R. E. and ST JOHN, N. H. (1966), *Social Class and the Urban School*, Wiley.

HOYLE, E. (1965), 'Organizational analysis in the field of education', *Educ. Research*, 7, pp. 97-114.

HOYLE, E. (1969), *The Role of the Teacher*, Routledge & Kegan Paul.

JACKSON, B. and MARSDEN, D. (1962), *Education and the Working Class*, Routledge & Kegan Paul.

JAY, L. J. (1966), 'The mobility of teachers', University of Sheffield, Department of Education (mimeographed).

KAHN, R. L. *et al.* (1964), *Organizational Stress: Studies in Role Conflict and Ambiguity*, Wiley.

142

KATZ, D. and KAHN, R. L. (1966), *The Social Psychology of Organizations,* Wiley.

KELSALL, R. K. and KELSALL, H. M. (1969), *The Schoolteacher in England and the United States,* Pergamon.

KING, R. A. (1969), *Values and Involvement in a Grammar School,* Routledge & Kegan Paul.

LAWLER, E. E. (1970), 'Job design and employee motivation' in Vroom, V. H. and Decci, E. L., *Management and Motivation,* Penguin.

LIEBERMAN, M. (1956), *Education as a Profession,* Prentice-Hall.

MANWILLER, L. V. (1958), 'Expectations regarding teachers', *J. Exp. Educ.,* 26, pp. 319-24.

MASLOW, A. H. (1943), 'A theory of human motivation', *Psychol. Review,* 50, pp. 370-96.

MASON, W. S., DRESSEL, R. J. and BAIN, R. K. (1959), 'Sex role and career orientations of beginning teachers', *Harvard Educ. Rev.,* 29, pp. 370-83.

MERTON, R. K. (1957), 'The role-set: problems in sociological theory', *Brit. J. Sociol.,* VIII(2), pp. 106-20.

MERTON, R. K., FISKE, M. and KENDALL, P. L. (1956), *The Focussed Interview,* Free Press.

MILES, M. B. (1969), 'Planned change and organizational health: figure and ground' in Carver, F. and Sergiovanni, T., *Organizations and Human Behaviour: Focus on Schools,* McGraw-Hill.

MORRIS, C. N. (1957), 'Career patterns of teachers' in Styles, L. J. (ed.), *The Teacher's Role in American Society,* Fourteenth Yearbook of the Dewey Society.

MUSGROVE, E. (1967), 'Teachers' role conflicts in the English grammar and secondary modern school', *Int. J. Educ. Sciences,* 2, pp. 61-8.

MUSGROVE, F. and TAYLOR, P. H. (1965), 'Teachers' and parents' conception of the teacher's role', *Brit. J. Educ. Psychol.,* XXXV(2), pp. 171-9.

MUSGROVE, F. and TAYLOR, P. H. (1969), *Society and the Teacher's Role,* Routledge & Kegan Paul.

NEILL, A. S. (1939), *The Problem Teacher,* Jenkins.

PARSONS, T. (1951), *The Social System,* Free Press.

PEDLEY, R. (1965), 'Teacher training: a new approach', *Education,* 4 June.

PETERSON, W. A. (1964), 'Age, teacher's role and the institutional setting' in Biddle, B. J. and Ellena, W. J., *Contemporary Research on Teacher Effectiveness,* Holt, Rinehart & Winston.

REX, J. (1961), *Key Problems of Sociological Theory,* Routledge & Kegan Paul.

RIESMAN, D. (1957), 'Teachers as a counter-cyclical influence', *School Review,* 65.

RIESMAN, D., GLAZER, N. and DENNEY, R. (1950), *The Lonely Crowd, a study of the changing American character,* Yale University Press.

RUDD, W. G. and WISEMAN, S. (1962), 'Sources of dissatisfaction among a group of teachers', *Brit. J. Educ. Psychol.,* 32, pp. 275-91.

RUGH, D. (1961), 'The American teacher—victim of role inflation', *J. Teacher Educ.,* XII (1), pp. 54-6.

SARBIN, T. R. (1954), 'Role theory' in Lindzey, G. (ed.), *Handbook of Social Psychology,* Addison-Wesley.

SEEMAN, M. (1953), 'Role conflict and ambivalence in leadership', *Am. Soc. Rev.,* XVIII, pp. 373-80.

SERGIOVANNI, T. J. (1969), 'Factors which affect satisfaction and dissatisfaction of teachers' in Carver, F. and Sergiovanni, T., *Organizations and Human Behavior: focus on schools,* McGraw-Hill.

SPINDLER, G. D. (ed.) (1963), *Education and Culture,* Holt, Rinehart & Winston.

TAYLOR, P. H. (1968), 'Teachers' role conflicts—II: English infant and junior schools', *Int. J. Educ. Sciences,* 2(3), pp. 167-73.

TAYLOR, W. (1963), *The Secondary Modern School,* Faber.

TAYLOR, W. (1969a), *Society and the Education of Teachers,* Faber.

TAYLOR, W. (ed.) (1969b), *Towards a Policy for the Education of Teachers,* Butterworths.

TOBY, J. (1952), 'Some variables in role conflict analysis', *Social Forces,* XXX, pp. 323-7.

TRIST, E. (1970), 'The professional facilitation of planned change in organisations' in Vroom, V. H. and Decci, E. L. (eds), *Management and Motivation,* Penguin.

TROPP, A. (1957), *The Schoolteachers,* Heinemann.

TURNER, C. M. (1969), 'An organisational analysis of a secondary modern school', *Soc. Rev.,* XVII (1), pp. 67-86.

VROOM, V. H. and DECCI, E. L. (eds) (1970), *Management and Motivation,* Penguin.

WALLER, W. (1965), *The Sociology of Teaching,* Wiley.

WARDWELL, W. (1955), 'The reduction of strain in a marginal social role', *Am. J. Soc.,* LXI, pp. 16-25.

WESTWOOD, L. J. (1967a), 'The role of the teacher—I', *Educ. Research,* IX(2), pp. 122-34.

WESTWOOD, L. J. (1967b), 'The role of the teacher—II', *Educ. Research,* X(1), pp. 21-37.

WILSON, B. R. (1962), 'The teacher's role: a sociological analysis', *Brit. J. Sociol.,* XIII (1), pp. 15-32.

WILSON, J., WILLIAMS, N. and SUGARMAN, B. (1967), *Introduction to Moral Education,* Penguin.

Index of names

145

Index of subjects

International Library of Sociology

Edited by
John Rex
University of Warwick

Founded by
Karl Mannheim

as The International Library of Sociology
and Social Reconstruction

*This Catalogue also contains other Social Science
series published by Routledge*

Routledge & Kegan Paul   London and Boston

68-74 Carter Lane London EC4V 5EL
9 Park Street Boston Mass 02108

Contents

● *Books so marked are available in paperback*
All books are in Metric Demy 8vo format (216 × 138mm approx.)

GENERAL SOCIOLOGY

Belshaw, Cyril. The Conditions of Social Performance. *An Exploratory Theory. 144 pp.*

Brown, Robert. Explanation in Social Science. *208 pp.*

● Rules and Laws in Sociology.

Cain, Maureen E. Society and the Policeman's Role. *About 300 pp.*

Gibson, Quentin. The Logic of Social Enquiry. *240 pp.*

Gurvitch, Georges. Sociology of Law. *Preface by Roscoe Pound. 264 pp.*

Homans, George C. Sentiments and Activities: *Essays in Social Science. 336 pp.*

Johnson, Harry M. Sociology: *a Systematic Introduction. Foreword by Robert K. Merton. 710 pp.*

Mannheim, Karl. Essays on Sociology and Social Psychology. *Edited by Paul Keckskemeti. With Editorial Note by Adolph Lowe. 344 pp.*

Systematic Sociology: *An Introduction to the Study of Society. Edited by J. S. Erös and Professor W. A. C. Stewart. 220 pp.*

Martindale, Don. The Nature and Types of Sociological Theory. *292 pp.*

● **Maus, Heinz.** A Short History of Sociology. *234 pp.*

Mey, Harald. Field-Theory. *A Study of its Application in the Social Sciences. 352 pp.*

Myrdal, Gunnar. Value in Social Theory: *A Collection of Essays on Methodology. Edited by Paul Streeten. 332 pp.*

Ogburn, William F., and **Nimkoff, Meyer F.** A Handbook of Sociology. *Preface by Karl Mannheim. 656 pp. 46 figures. 35 tables.*

Parsons, Talcott, and **Smelser, Neil J.** Economy and Society: *A Study in the Integration of Economic and Social Theory. 362 pp.*

● **Rex, John.** Key Problems of Sociological Theory. *220 pp.*

Urry, John. Reference Groups and the Theory of Revolution.

FOREIGN CLASSICS OF SOCIOLOGY

● **Durkheim, Emile.** Suicide. *A Study in Sociology. Edited and with an Introduction by George Simpson. 404 pp.*

Professional Ethics and Civic Morals. *Translated by Cornelia Brookfield. 288 pp.*

● **Gerth, H. H.,** and **Mills, C. Wright.** From Max Weber: *Essays in Sociology. 502 pp.*

Tönnies, Ferdinand. Community and Association. *(Gemeinschaft und Gesellschaft.) Translated and Supplemented by Charles P. Loomis. Foreword by Pitirim A. Sorokin. 334 pp.*

SOCIAL STRUCTURE

Andreski, Stanislav. Military Organization and Society. *Foreword by Professor A. R. Radcliffe-Brown. 226 pp. 1 folder.*

Coontz, Sydney H. Population Theories and the Economic Interpretation. *202 pp.*

Coser, Lewis. The Functions of Social Conflict. *204 pp.*

Dickie-Clark, H. F. Marginal Situation: *A Sociological Study of a Coloured Group. 240 pp. 11 tables.*

Glass, D. V. (Ed.). Social Mobility in Britain. *Contributions by J. Berent, T. Bottomore, R. C. Chambers, J. Floud, D. V. Glass, J. R. Hall, H. T. Himmelweit, R. K. Kelsall, F. M. Martin, C. A. Moser, R. Mukherjee, and W. Ziegel. 420 pp.*

Glaser, Barney, and **Strauss, Anselm L.** Status Passage. *A Formal Theory. 208 pp.*

Jones, Garth N. Planned Organizational Change: *An Exploratory Study Using an Empirical Approach. 268 pp.*

Kelsall, R. K. Higher Civil Servants in Britain: *From 1870 to the Present Day. 268 pp. 31 tables.*

König, René. The Community. *232 pp. Illustrated.*

● **Lawton, Denis.** Social Class, Language and Education. *192 pp.*

McLeish, John. The Theory of Social Change: *Four Views Considered. 128 pp.*

Marsh, David C. The Changing Social Structure of England and Wales, 1871-1961. *288 pp.*

Mouzelis, Nicos. Organization and Bureaucracy. *An Analysis of Modern Theories. 240 pp.*

Mulkay, M. J. Functionalism, Exchange and Theoretical Strategy. *272 pp.*

Ossowski, Stanislaw. Class Structure in the Social Consciousness. *210 pp.*

SOCIOLOGY AND POLITICS

Hertz, Frederick. Nationality in History and Politics: *A Psychology and Sociology of National Sentiment and Nationalism. 432 pp.*

Kornhauser, William. The Politics of Mass Society. *272 pp. 20 tables.*

Laidler, Harry W. History of Socialism. *Social-Economic Movements: An Historical and Comparative Survey of Socialism, Communism, Co-operation, Utopianism; and other Systems of Reform and Reconstruction. 992 pp.*

Mannheim, Karl. Freedom, Power and Democratic Planning. *Edited by Hans Gerth and Ernest K. Bramstedt. 424 pp.*

Mansur, Fatma. Process of Independence. *Foreword by A. H. Hanson. 208 pp.*

Martin, David A. Pacificism: *an Historical and Sociological Study. 262 pp.*

Myrdal, Gunnar. The Political Element in the Development of Economic Theory. *Translated from the German by Paul Streeten. 282 pp.*

Wootton, Graham. Workers, Unions and the State. *188 pp.*

FOREIGN AFFAIRS: THEIR SOCIAL, POLITICAL AND ECONOMIC FOUNDATIONS

Mayer, J. P. Political Thought in France from the Revolution to the Fifth Republic. *164 pp.*

CRIMINOLOGY

Ancel, Marc. Social Defence: *A Modern Approach to Criminal Problems. Foreword by Leon Radzinowicz. 240 pp.*

Cloward, Richard A., and **Ohlin, Lloyd E.** Delinquency and Opportunity: *A Theory of Delinquent Gangs. 248 pp.*

Downes, David M. The Delinquent Solution. *A Study in Subcultural Theory. 296 pp.*

Dunlop, A. B., and **McCabe, S.** Young Men in Detention Centres. *192 pp.*

Friedlander, Kate. The Psycho-Analytical Approach to Juvenile Delinquency: *Theory, Case Studies, Treatment. 320 pp.*

Glueck, Sheldon, and **Eleanor.** Family Environment and Delinquency. *With the statistical assistance of Rose W. Kneznek. 340 pp.*

Lopez-Rey, Manuel. Crime. *An Analytical Appraisal. 288 pp.*

Mannheim, Hermann. Comparative Criminology: *a Text Book. Two volumes. 442 pp. and 380 pp.*

Morris, Terence. The Criminal Area: *A Study in Social Ecology. Foreword by Hermann Mannheim. 232 pp. 25 tables. 4 maps.*

● **Taylor, Ian, Walton, Paul,** and **Young, Jock.** The New Criminology. *For a Social Theory of Deviance.*

SOCIAL PSYCHOLOGY

Bagley, Christopher. The Social Psychology of the Epileptic Child. *320 pp.*

Barbu, Zevedei. Problems of Historical Psychology. *248 pp.*

Blackburn, Julian. Psychology and the Social Pattern. *184 pp.*

● **Brittan, Arthur.** Meanings and Situations. *224 pp.*

● **Fleming, C. M.** Adolescence: Its Social Psychology. *With an Introduction to recent findings from the fields of Anthropology, Physiology, Medicine, Psychometrics and Sociometry. 288 pp.*

● The Social Psychology of Education: *An Introduction and Guide to Its Study. 136 pp.*

Homans, George C. The Human Group. *Foreword by Bernard DeVoto. Introduction by Robert K. Merton. 526 pp.*

Social Behaviour: *its Elementary Forms. 416 pp.*

Klein, Josephine. The Study of Groups. *226 pp. 31 figures. 5 tables.*

Linton, Ralph. The Cultural Background of Personality. *132 pp.*

Mayo, Elton. The Social Problems of an Industrial Civilization. *With an appendix on the Political Problem. 180 pp.*

Ottaway, A. K. C. Learning Through Group Experience. *176 pp.*

Ridder, J. C. de. The Personality of the Urban African in South Africa. *A Thematic Apperception Test Study. 196 pp. 12 plates.*

● **Rose, Arnold M.** (Ed.). Human Behaviour and Social Processes: *an Interactionist Approach. Contributions by Arnold M. Rose, Ralph H. Turner, Anselm Strauss, Everett C. Hughes, E. Franklin Frazier, Howard S. Becker, et al. 696 pp.*

Smelser, Neil J. Theory of Collective Behaviour. *448 pp.*

Stephenson, Geoffrey M. The Development of Conscience. *128 pp.*

Young, Kimball. Handbook of Social Psychology. *658 pp. 16 figures. 10 tables.*

SOCIOLOGY OF THE FAMILY

Banks, J. A. Prosperity and Parenthood: *A Study of Family Planning among The Victorian Middle Classes. 262 pp.*

Bell, Colin R. Middle Class Families: *Social and Geographical Mobility. 224 pp.*

Burton, Lindy. Vulnerable Children. *272 pp.*

Gavron, Hannah. The Captive Wife: *Conflicts of Household Mothers. 190 pp.*

George, Victor, and **Wilding, Paul.** Motherless Families. *220 pp.*

Klein, Josephine. Samples from English Cultures.
1. Three Preliminary Studies and Aspects of Adult Life in England. *447 pp.*
2. Child-Rearing Practices and Index. *247 pp.*

Klein, Viola. Britain's Married Women Workers. *180 pp.*
The Feminine Character. *History of an Ideology. 244 pp.*

McWhinnie, Alexina M. Adopted Children. *How They Grow Up. 304 pp.*

Myrdal, Alva, and **Klein, Viola.** Women's Two Roles: *Home and Work. 238 pp. 27 tables.*

Parsons, Talcott, and **Bales, Robert F.** Family: Socialization and Interaction Process. *In collaboration with James Olds, Morris Zelditch and Philip E. Slater. 456 pp. 50 figures and tables.*

SOCIAL SERVICES

Bastide, Roger. The Sociology of Mental Disorder. *Translated from the French by Jean McNeil. 260 pp.*

Carlebach, Julius. Caring For Children in Trouble. *266 pp.*

Forder, R. A. (Ed.). Penelope Hall's Social Services of England and Wales. *352 pp.*

George, Victor. Foster Care. *Theory and Practice. 234 pp.*
Social Security: *Beveridge and After. 258 pp.*

● **Goetschius, George W.** Working with Community Groups. *256 pp.*

Goetschius, George W., and **Tash, Joan.** Working with Unattached Youth. *416 pp.*

Hall, M. P., and **Howes, I. V.** The Church in Social Work. *A Study of Moral Welfare Work undertaken by the Church of England. 320 pp.*

Heywood, Jean S. Children in Care: *the Development of the Service for the Deprived Child. 264 pp.*

Hoenig, J., and **Hamilton, Marian W.** The De-Segration of the Mentally Ill. *284 pp.*

Jones, Kathleen. Mental Health and Social Policy, 1845-1959. *264 pp.*

King, Roy D., Raynes, Norma V., and **Tizard, Jack.** Patterns of Residential Care. *356 pp.*

Leigh, John. Young People and Leisure. *256 pp.*

Morris, Mary. Voluntary Work and the Welfare State. *300 pp.*

Morris, Pauline. Put Away: *A Sociological Study of Institutions for the Mentally Retarded. 364 pp.*

Nokes, P. L. The Professional Task in Welfare Practice. *152 pp.*

Timms, Noel. Psychiatric Social Work in Great Britain (1939-1962). *280 pp.*

● Social Casework: *Principles and Practice. 256 pp.*

Young, A. F., and **Ashton, E. T.** British Social Work in the Nineteenth Century. *288 pp.*

Young, A. F. Social Services in British Industry. *272 pp.*

SOCIOLOGY OF EDUCATION

Banks, Olive. Parity and Prestige in English Secondary Education: a Study in Educational Sociology. *272 pp.*

Bentwich, Joseph. Education in Israel. *224 pp. 8 pp. plates.*

● **Blyth, W. A. L.** English Primary Education. *A Sociological Description.*
   1. Schools. *232 pp.*
   2. Background. *168 pp.*

Collier, K. G. The Social Purposes of Education: *Personal and Social Values in Education. 268 pp.*

Dale, R. R., and **Griffith, S.** Down Stream: *Failure in the Grammar School. 108 pp.*

Dore, R. P. Education in Tokugawa Japan. *356 pp. 9 pp. plates*

Evans, K. M. Sociometry and Education. *158 pp.*

Foster, P. J. Education and Social Change in Ghana. *336 pp. 3 maps.*

Fraser, W. R. Education and Society in Modern France. *150 pp.*

Grace, Gerald R. Role Conflict and the Teacher. *About 200 pp.*

Hans, Nicholas. New Trends in Education in the Eighteenth Century. *278 pp. 19 tables.*

● Comparative Education: *A Study of Educational Factors and Traditions. 360 pp.*

Hargreaves, David. Interpersonal Relations and Education. *432 pp.*

● Social Relations in a Secondary School. *240 pp.*

Holmes, Brian. Problems in Education. *A Comparative Approach. 336 pp.*

King, Ronald. Values and Involvement in a Grammar School. *164 pp.*
   School Organization and Pupil Involvement. *A Study of Secondary Schools.*

● **Mannheim, Karl**, and **Stewart, W. A. C.** An Introduction to the Sociology of Education. *206 pp.*

Morris, Raymond N. The Sixth Form and College Entrance. *231 pp.*

● **Musgrove, F.** Youth and the Social Order. *176 pp.*

● **Ottaway, A. K. C.** Education and Society: An Introduction to the Sociology of Education. *With an Introduction by W. O. Lester Smith. 212 pp.*

Peers, Robert. Adult Education: *A Comparative Study. 398 pp.*

Pritchard, D. G. Education and the Handicapped: *1760 to 1960. 258 pp.*
Richardson, Helen. Adolescent Girls in Approved Schools. *308 pp.*
Stratta, Erica. The Education of Borstal Boys. *A Study of their Educational Experiences prior to, and during Borstal Training. 256 pp.*

SOCIOLOGY OF CULTURE

Eppel, E. M., and **M.** Adolescents and Morality: *A Study of some Moral Values and Dilemmas of Working Adolescents in the Context of a changing Climate of Opinion. Foreword by W. J. H. Sprott. 268 pp. 39 tables.*
● **Fromm, Erich.** The Fear of Freedom. *286 pp.*
  The Sane Society. *400 pp.*
Mannheim, Karl. Essays on the Sociology of Culture. *Edited by Ernst Mannheim in co-operation with Paul Kecskemeti. Editorial Note by Adolph Lowe. 280 pp.*
Weber, Alfred. Farewell to European History: *or The Conquest of Nihilism Translated from the German by R. F. C. Hull. 224 pp.*

SOCIOLOGY OF RELIGION

Argyle, Michael. Religious Behaviour. *224 pp. 8 figures. 41 tables.*
Nelson, G. K. Spiritualism and Society. *313 pp.*
Stark, Werner. The Sociology of Religion. *A Study of Christendom.*
  Volume I. *Established Religion. 248 pp.*
  Volume II. *Sectarian Religion. 368 pp.*
  Volume III. *The Universal Church. 464 pp.*
  Volume IV. *Types of Religious Man. 352 pp.*
  Volume V. *Types of Religious Culture. 464 pp.*
Watt, W. Montgomery. Islam and the Integration of Society. *320 pp.*

SOCIOLOGY OF ART AND LITERATURE

Jarvie, Ian C. Towards a Sociology of the Cinema. *A Comparative Essay on the Structure and Functioning of a Major Entertainment Industry. 405 pp.*
Rust, Frances S. Dance in Society. *An Analysis of the Relationships between the Social Dance and Society in England from the Middle Ages to the Present Day. 256 pp. 8 pp. of plates.*
Schücking, L. L. The Sociology of Literary Taste. *112 pp.*

SOCIOLOGY OF KNOWLEDGE

Mannheim, Karl. Essays on the Sociology of Knowledge. *Edited by Paul Kecskemeti. Editorial Note by Adolph Lowe. 353 pp.*

Remmling, Gunter W. (Ed.). Towards the Sociology of Knowledge. *Origins and Development of a Sociological Thought Style.*

Stark, Werner. The Sociology of Knowledge: *An Essay in Aid of a Deeper Understanding of the History of Ideas. 384 pp.*

URBAN SOCIOLOGY

Ashworth, William. The Genesis of Modern British Town Planning: *A Study in Economic and Social History of the Nineteenth and Twentieth Centuries. 288 pp.*

Cullingworth, J. B. Housing Needs and Planning Policy: *A Restatement of the Problems of Housing Need and 'Overspill' in England and Wales. 232 pp. 44 tables. 8 maps.*

Dickinson, Robert E. City and Region: *A Geographical Interpretation. 608 pp. 125 figures.*

The West European City: *A Geographical Interpretation. 600 pp. 129 maps. 29 plates.*

● The City Region in Western Europe. *320 pp. Maps.*

Humphreys, Alexander J. New Dubliners: *Urbanization and the Irish Family. Foreword by George C. Homans. 304 pp.*

Jackson, Brian. Working Class Community: *Some General Notions raised by a Series of Studies in Northern England. 192 pp.*

Jennings, Hilda. Societies in the Making: *a Study of Development and Redevelopment within a County Borough. Foreword by D. A. Clark. 286 pp.*

● **Mann, P. H.** An Approach to Urban Sociology. *240 pp.*

Morris, R. N., and **Mogey, J.** The Sociology of Housing. *Studies at Berinsfield. 232 pp. 4 pp. plates.*

Rosser, C., and **Harris, C.** The Family and Social Change. *A Study of Family and Kinship in a South Wales Town. 352 pp. 8 maps.*

RURAL SOCIOLOGY

Chambers, R. J. H. Settlement Schemes in Tropical Africa: *A Selective Study. 268 pp.*

Haswell, M. R. The Economics of Development in Village India. *120 pp.*

Littlejohn, James. Westrigg: *the Sociology of a Cheviot Parish. 172 pp. 5 figures.*

Mayer, Adrian C. Peasants in the Pacific. *A Study of Fiji Indian Rural Society. 248 pp. 20 plates.*

Williams, W. M. The Sociology of an English Village: *Gosforth. 272 pp. 12 figures. 13 tables.*

SOCIOLOGY OF INDUSTRY AND DISTRIBUTION

Anderson, Nels. Work and Leisure. *280 pp.*
● **Blau, Peter M.**, and **Scott, W. Richard.** Formal Organizations: *a Comparative approach. Introduction and Additional Bibliography by J. H. Smith. 326 pp.*
Eldridge, J. E. T. Industrial Disputes. *Essays in the Sociology of Industrial Relations. 288 pp.*
Hetzler, Stanley. Applied Measures for Promoting Technological Growth. *352 pp.*
Technological Growth and Social Change. *Achieving Modernization. 269 pp.*
Hollowell, Peter G. The Lorry Driver. *272 pp.*
Jefferys, Margot, *with the assistance of Winifred Moss.* Mobility in the Labour Market: *Employment Changes in Battersea and Dagenham. Preface by Barbara Wootton. 186 pp. 51 tables.*
Millerson, Geoffrey. The Qualifying Associations: *a Study in Professionalization. 320 pp.*
Smelser, Neil J. Social Change in the Industrial Revolution: *An Application of Theory to the Lancashire Cotton Industry, 1770-1840. 468 pp. 12 figures. 14 tables.*
Williams, Gertrude. Recruitment to Skilled Trades. *240 pp.*
Young, A. F. Industrial Injuries Insurance: *an Examination of British Policy. 192 pp.*

DOCUMENTARY

Schlesinger, Rudolf (Ed.). Changing Attitudes in Soviet Russia.
2. The Nationalities Problem and Soviet Administration. *Selected Readings on the Development of Soviet Nationalities Policies. Introduced by the editor. Translated by W. W. Gottlieb. 324 pp.*

ANTHROPOLOGY

Ammar, Hamed. Growing up in an Egyptian Village: *Silwa, Province of Aswan. 336 pp.*
Brandel-Syrier, Mia. Reeftown Elite. *A Study of Social Mobility in a Modern African Community on the Reef. 376 pp.*
Crook, David, and **Isabel.** Revolution in a Chinese Village: *Ten Mile Inn. 230 pp. 8 plates. 1 map.*
Dickie-Clark, H. F. The Marginal Situation. *A Sociological Study of a Coloured Group. 236 pp.*
Dube, S. C. Indian Village. *Foreword by Morris Edward Opler. 276 pp. 4 plates.*
India's Changing Villages: *Human Factors in Community Development. 260 pp. 8 plates. 1 map.*

Firth, Raymond. Malay Fishermen. *Their Peasant Economy. 420 pp. 17 pp. plates.*

Gulliver, P. H. Social Control in an African Society: a Study of the Arusha, Agricultural Masai of Northern Tanganyika. *320 pp. 8 plates. 10 figures.*

Ishwaran, K. Shivapur. *A South Indian Village. 216 pp.*
Tradition and Economy in Village India: *An Interactionist Approach. Foreword by Conrad Arensburg. 176 pp.*

Jarvie, Ian C. The Revolution in Anthropology. *268 pp.*

Jarvie, Ian C., and **Agassi, Joseph.** Hong Kong. *A Society in Transition. 396 pp. Illustrated with plates and maps.*

Little, Kenneth L. Mende of Sierra Leone. *308 pp. and folder.*
Negroes in Britain. *With a New Introduction and Contemporary Study by Leonard Bloom. 320 pp.*

Lowie, Robert H. Social Organization. *494 pp.*

Mayer, Adrian C. Caste and Kinship in Central India: *A Village and its Region. 328 pp. 16 plates. 15 figures. 16 tables.*

Smith, Raymond T. The Negro Family in British Guiana: *Family Structure and Social Status in the Villages. With a Foreword by Meyer Fortes. 314 pp. 8 plates. 1 figure. 4 maps.*

SOCIOLOGY AND PHILOSOPHY

Barnsley, John H. The Social Reality of Ethics. *A Comparative Analysis of Moral Codes. 448 pp.*

Diesing, Paul. Patterns of Discovery in the Social Sciences. *362 pp.*

Douglas, Jack D. (Ed.). Understanding Everyday Life. *Toward the Reconstruction of Sociological Knowledge. Contributions by Alan F. Blum. Aaron W. Cicourel, Norman K. Denzin, Jack D. Douglas, John Heeren, Peter McHugh, Peter K. Manning, Melvin Power, Matthew Speier, Roy Turner, D. Lawrence Wieder, Thomas P. Wilson and Don H. Zimmerman. 370 pp.*

Jarvie, Ian C. Concepts and Society. *216 pp.*

Roche, Maurice. Phenomenology, Language and the Social Sciences. *About 400 pp.*

Sahay, Arun. Sociological Analysis.

Sklair, Leslie. The Sociology of Progress. *320 pp.*

International Library of Anthropology
General Editor Adam Kuper

Brown, Raula. The Chimbu. *A Study of Change in the New Guinea Highlands.*
Van Den Berghe, Pierre L. Power and Privilege at an African University.

International Library of Social Policy

General Editor Kathleen Jones

Holman, Robert. Trading in Children. *A Study of Private Fostering.*
Jones, Kathleen. History of the Mental Health Services. *428 pp.*
Thomas, J. E. The English Prison Officer since 1850: *A Study in Conflict.*
 258 pp.

Primary Socialization, Language and Education

General Editor Basil Bernstein

Bernstein, Basil. Class, Codes and Control. *2 volumes.*
 1. *Theoretical Studies Towards a Sociology of Language. 254 pp.*
 2. *Applied Studies Towards a Sociology of Language. About 400 pp.*
Brandis, Walter, and **Henderson, Dorothy.** Social Class, Language and
 Communication. *288 pp.*
Cook-Gumperz, Jenny. Social Control and Socialization. *A Study of Class
 Differences in the Language of Maternal Control.*
Gahagan, D. M., and **G. A.** Talk Reform. *Exploration in Language for Infant
 School Children. 160 pp.*
Robinson, W. P., and **Rackstraw, Susan, D. A.** A Question of Answers.
 2 volumes. 192 pp. and 180 pp.
Turner, Geoffrey, J., and **Mohan, Bernard, A.** A Linguistic Description and
 Computer Programme for Children's Speech. *208 pp.*

Reports of the Institute of Community Studies

Cartwright, Ann. Human Relations and Hospital Care. *272 pp.*
 Parents and Family Planning Services. *306 pp.*
 Patients and their Doctors. *A Study of General Practice. 304 pp.*
● **Jackson, Brian.** Streaming: *an Education System in Miniature. 168 pp.*
Jackson, Brian, and **Marsden, Dennis.** Education and the Working Class:
 *Some General Themes raised by a Study of 88 Working-class Children
 in a Northern Industrial City. 268 pp. 2 folders.*
Marris, Peter. The Experience of Higher Education. *232 pp. 27 tables.*
Marris, Peter, and **Rein, Martin.** Dilemmas of Social Reform. *Poverty and
 Community Action in the United States. 256 pp.*
Marris, Peter, and **Somerset, Anthony.** African Businessmen. *A Study of
 Entrepreneurship and Development in Kenya. 256 pp.*
Mills, Richard. Young Outsiders: *a Study in Alternative Communities.*

Runciman, W. G. Relative Deprivation and Social Justice. *A Study of Attitudes to Social Inequality in Twentieth Century England. 352 pp.*

Townsend, Peter. The Family Life of Old People: *An Inquiry in East London. Foreword by J. H. Sheldon. 300 pp. 3 figures. 63 tables.*

Willmott, Peter. Adolescent Boys in East London. *230 pp.*
The Evolution of a Community: *a study of Dagenham after forty years. 168 pp. 2 maps.*

Willmott, Peter, and **Young, Michael.** Family and Class in a London Suburb. *202 pp. 47 tables.*

Young, Michael. Innovation and Research in Education. *192 pp.*

● **Young, Michael,** and **McGeeney, Patrick.** Learning Begins at Home. *A Study of a Junior School and its Parents. 128 pp.*

Young, Michael, and **Willmott, Peter.** Family and Kinship in East London. *Foreword by Richard M. Titmuss. 252 pp. 39 tables.*
The Symmetrical Family.

Reports of the Institute for Social Studies in Medical Care

Cartwright, Ann, Hockey, Lisbeth, and **Anderson, John L.** Life Before Death.

Dunnell, Karen, and **Cartwright, Ann.** Medicine Takers, Prescribers and Hoarders. *190 pp.*

Medicine, Illness and Society
General Editor W. M. Williams

Robinson, David. The Process of Becoming Ill.

Stacey, Margaret. *et al.* Hospitals, Children and Their Families. *The Report of a Pilot Study. 202 pp.*

Monographs in Social Theory
General Editor Arthur Brittan

Bauman, Zygmunt. Culture as Praxis.

Dixon, Keith. Sociological Theory. *Pretence and Possibility.*

Smith, Anthony D. The Concept of Social Change. *A Critique of the Functionalist Theory of Social Change.*

13

Routledge Social Science Journals

The British Journal of Sociology. *Edited by Terence P. Morris. Vol. 1, No. 1, March 1950 and Quarterly. Roy. 8vo. Back numbers available. An international journal with articles on all aspects of sociology.*

Economy and Society. *Vol. 1, No. 1. February 1972 and Quarterly. Metric Roy. 8vo. A journal for all social scientists covering sociology, philosophy, anthropology, economics and history. Back numbers available.*

Year Book of Social Policy in Britain, The. *Edited by Kathleen Jones. 1971. Published Annually.*

Printed in Great Britain by Lewis Reprints Limited
Brown Knight & Truscott Group, London and Tonbridge

1373

14